M000279991

α

Needle-made
L·A·C·E·S

PAT EARNSHAW

Needle-made
L·A·C·E·S

MATERIALS

DESIGNS

TECHNIQUES

Ward Lock Limited · London

© Text and Illustrations Pat Earnshaw 1988
© Photography Ward Lock Limited 1988

First published in Great Britain in 1988
by Ward Lock Limited, 8 Clifford Street,
London W1X 1RB, an Egmont Company.

All Rights Reserved. No part of this publication
may be reproduced, stored in a retrieval system,
or transmitted, in any form or by any means,
electronic, mechanical, phototcopying, record-
ing, or otherwise, without the prior permission
of the Copyright owners.

Designed by Melissa Orrom
Artwork by Ann Winterbotham
Photography by Jon Bouchier
Text set in Horley Old Style
by Multiplex Techniques Ltd, St Mary Cray,
Kent.

Printed and bound in Great Britain by Hazell,
Watson and Viney Ltd, Aylesbury

The publishers would like to thank the Rauman
Museum in Finland for their kind permission
to reproduce the photographs on page 89.

British Library Cataloguing in Publication Data
Earnshaw, Pat
  Needle-made laces.
  1. Needlepoint lace
  I. Title
  746.2′2   ˈTT800

  ISBN 0-7063-6620-4

Cover photograph: Detail of a flounce of point de France, third quarter of the seventeenth century (magnification × 1½). The solid areas show detached buttonhole stitch with a straight return, closed form.

CONTENTS

INTRODUCTION

*L*ACE is essentially a lightweight arrangement of threads worked together in such a way that they enclose a series of holes. The process of moving the threads to make the holes usually involves the use of implements.

Where several threads are to be worked bobbins, or thread holders, are used. A number of threads – between 8 and 1,000 – are suspended from pins, or over a support, so that they hang downwards. They are then either:

(i) Twisted around and crossed over each other (bobbin laces); or

(ii) knotted together (macramé).

When only a single thread is involved, the implement used can be:

(i) a hook making chain-stitch (crochet and tambour embroidery on net);

(ii) a shuttle making larkshead knots (tatting);

(iii) a shuttle-and-gauge making sheet-bend knots (filet);

(iv) knitting needles making chain-stitch style loops in a horizontal sequence (knitting);

(v) the sewing needle (needle-made laces). The sewing needle is infinitely the most versatile single-thread implement, in spite of what might be regarded as a serious initial disadvantage – that it can operate only with short lengths of thread and must be constantly replenished. The variable movements of the sewing needle and its single thread, making stitches to create laces, forms the subject of this book. *Needle-made Laces* describes twelve distinct projects based on different ways of using the needle.

Embroidered laces (Chapters 1 and 2). The lace is made by changing the nature of a pre-existing woven cloth so that holes are created in a solid fabric by the movements of the threads (Drawnwork; Cutwork; Greek lace; Ruskin lace; Richelieu work; Intagliatela; Carrickmacross guipure; Broderie anglaise; Ladderwork; Ayrshire work).

Needle, Needlepoint or Buttonhole stitch laces (Chapters 3, 4 and 5). Looping stitches are the main and often the only ones used; they include all types of buttonhole stitch (Reticella; Aemilia Ars; Punto in aria; Venetian, French and Belgian laces; Hollie point, English Needle Lace).

Mixed laces (Chapters 6 and 7). Buttonhole and sometimes other needle-made stitches are combined with areas which are either darned or pre-woven (Halas; Tape- or Braid-based laces).

Knotted laces (Chapter 8). The lace is composed entirely of a limited range of knots (Puncetto; Arab; Palestine; Armenian; Bebilla).

Needlewoven laces with some knotting (Chapter 9). (Teneriffe and other spider-web laces).

Embroidered gauze or machine net (Chapters 10, 11 and 12). Solid areas are produced in an openwork fabric, instead of openworks being produced in a solid fabric, as was the case with the embroidered laces (Buratto; Limerick needle-run; Carrickmacross appliqué, Carrickmacross guipure, net-on-net, gauze-on-net).

In each chapter directions are given for making the type of lace stated, with details of the setting up, the order of working and the stitches used. Variations are listed briefly, indicating different methods of approach, or stitches used, in laces closely related to the main project. For example, in Chapter 4, Venetian Laces, the variations of French Alençon and Argentan and the Brussels Point de gaze are given. The final appearance of these laces is quite distinctive, but the actual method of working is remarkably similar to Venetian. The directions for making serve an additional purpose: the technique of making the lace is also the main way by which the finished laces can be identified. Creation and recognition go hand in hand.

Materials The options are left open to give scope for personal preference and ability, but suggestions are made at the beginning of each chapter. Further advice can be obtained from the suppliers listed at the end of the book.

Note that cellulose sheeting either tinted or clear, can be substituted for the recommended architect's linen.

Thread The traditional off-white of antique linen laces from the sixteenth century onwards was always to some extent offset by the use of coloured silks. The wide range of threads available today — cotton, mercerized cotton, linen, wool, silk and polyesters, white or dyed — gives a vast freedom of choice for both traditionalists and innovators. Similarly, the traditional fine texture of most sixteenth-, seventeenth-, eighteenth- and nineteenth- century threads is a joy to experience from the past, but not an obligation to continue in the present. It is often better to begin with thick thread while you practice the stitches. Once the movements are mastered it is easy to progress to finer and finer work if your inclination leads you that way.

Needles Generally a blunt-tipped needle is used. This reduces the risk of going through the threads instead of through the spaces between them, and so speeds up the work. A pointed needle may be needed in addition.

As you make the stitches, turn the needle very slightly to prevent the untwisting or overtwisting of the spin, which causes the thread to curl on itself. In the seventeenth and eighteenth centuries, when extremely fine thread and therefore very fine needles were used, the fingers and thumbs of both hands were protected by thimbles to reduce the risk of punctured skin.

Line drawings Details of techniques are taken from actual laces, mainly nineteenth century or earlier.

In the buttonhole stitch laces, instructions are given in the Italian manner, that is starting at the bottom and working primarily from left to right with the needle pointed away from you. This gives better lighting of the stitches and more control of tension. If you prefer the reverse direction of working, from top to bottom with the needle towards you, simply turn the book round so that the figures are upside down. To reverse the stitch direction, trace off the line drawing, then turn the tracing paper over, so that you are looking at its reverse side. Left-right then becomes right-left, and vice versa.

In the diagrams included in the text to show how the various stitches are worked, the thread going to the needle's eye has been deliberately shortened so that unnecessary lines do not obscure the essential stitch movements.

The aim of *Needle-made Laces* is to present basic instructions, comprehensible to a beginner, in all types of lace traditionally made with a sewing needle. Books providing additional patterns and stitches and, in some cases, more advanced work are listed in the Bibliography (page 140).

1
DRAWNWORK

DRAWNWORK is a general term for the drawing out or pulling together of the threads of a plain-weave fabric in order to make holes and so convert it into an openwork: the antique name was *punto tirato* from the Italian *tirare*, meaning to pull or draw. Five methods are described in this chapter. A sixth method, Mexican drawnwork, is dealt with in Chapter 9, page 111.

◇DISTRIBUTION   Drawnwork has been made in every European country as well as in the Middle East, China, India, the Philippines, Mexico and South America. The different areas show minor variations of technique as well as major variations of design.

◇HISTORY   Drawnwork has an ancient origin, and examples have been found in Egypt dating back to pre-Christian times. Unlike many lace techniques, it has always had a decorative rather than a utilitarian function.

◇MATERIALS   An even-weave linen, with equal numbers of warps and wefts per square centimetre. It should be closely woven for methods 1 to 4, and loosely woven for method 5.

The work depends on the counting of threads, so match the fineness or coarseness of the even-weave fabric to your eyesight, patience and the time available.

A blunt-tipped needle for the main work, and a pointed needle for running in the ends.

A fairly fine twisted thread for strengthening the meshes, and thicker more loosely-spun threads, such as coloured silk strands, for the solid areas of the design.

Some means of supporting the work, for example an embroidery frame or a piece of softboard, to which the cloth can be fixed. If necessary, place dark paper beneath the linen so that the threads show up more clearly.

◇STITCHES   These are varied and will be described as they occur.

Method 1

Warps and wefts are drawn out right across the fabric, turning it into a meshwork onto which a design is then worked. Found in fifteenth-century Sicily (*disfilato*) and twentieth-century Brazil.

Preparation of the fabric

The edges of the cloth must be left raw all round so that threads can be taken completely out. Mark the size of the square or rectangle required with tacking stitches, using a coloured thread so that the lines show up clearly. These lines form the margins of the work.

Starting at the left-hand margin, draw out groups of warps at intervals: take four out, leave three, four out, leave three, and so on until the right-hand margin is reached (see fig. 1a). Turn the cloth through 90° and draw out wefts in the same way at the same intervals, starting at the left-hand margin and stopping at the right-hand (fig. 1b).

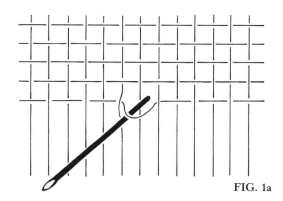

FIG. 1a

1a *To draw out a thread, insert the blunt tip of the needle under it, near the middle area, and pull gently until the thread is entirely removed.*

As the threads are removed, the kinks in the remaining strands will straighten out. Small residues of the original cloth will remain where warps and wefts intersect. This is a useful way of identifying the Drawnwork technique in a finished lace.

FIG. 1b

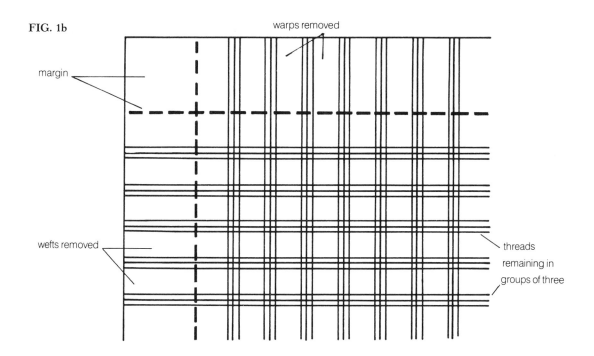

margin

warps removed

wefts removed

threads remaining in groups of three

1b *The final effect is of square holes over the entire cloth, except at the margins.*

FIG. 2

2 *A pattern for Drawnwork: the white blocks represent the solid areas of design; and the white lines are the square meshworks of residual warps and wefts which form the background.*

The design

Antique designs were often very elaborate, showing grotesque animals, fountains, putti, peacocks and flowers. However, some were simpler, such as fig. 2 which is taken from the Venetian Vinciolo's pattern book of 1606. This is the pattern to be worked for method 1. In some cases a pattern outline can be marked in ink on the meshes. If this cannot de done, the meshes must be counted throughout.

The two stitches most commonly used for working the design are:

Running stitch The needle is passed in and out of the meshes in one direction only.

Darning stitch The needle is passed in and out of the meshes horizontally and then vertically so that an effect of weaving or darning is produced (figs. 3a–c).

To work the pattern, begin at the left-hand bottom corner, two squares in and two squares up. Fill in the four-mesh block with running or darning stitch as preferred. The entire pattern is worked in this way. Whenever a thread has to be taken across a space, run it along the line of a warp or weft so that it will be caught in with the other threads when the ground is worked.

Working the ground

When all the design has been completed, start on the ground. The remaining warps and wefts are frail and unstable, and are overcast to strengthen them (figs. 4a–c).

FIG. 3a

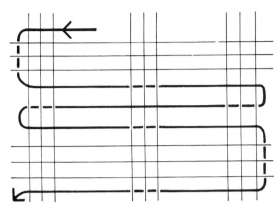

FIG. 3b

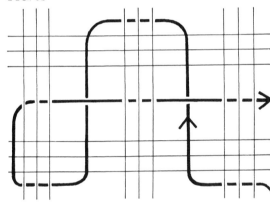

FIG. 3c

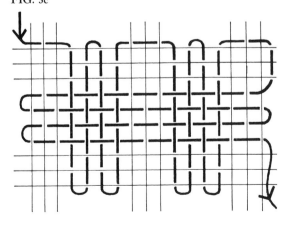

3a–c *Three methods of filling in the meshes.*

4 *Overcasting the remaining warps and wefts.*

FIG. 4a

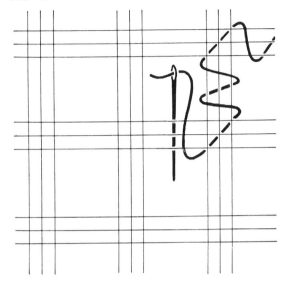

FIG. 4b

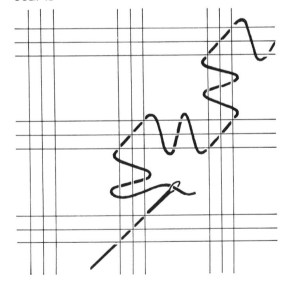

4a and b *Begin in one corner and work in a diagonal direction in a step-like manner, making two twists around a vertical bar, then two twists around a horizontal bar, vertical, horizontal, and so on, with the needle passing under the intersection each time.*

(cont. overleaf.)

FIG. 4c

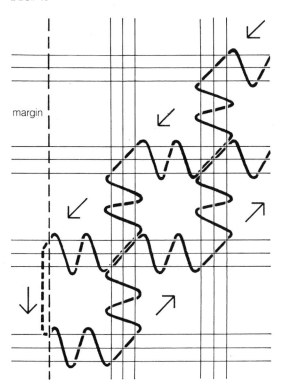

margin

4c *When the margin or, alternatively, the edge of the design, is reached, turn the cloth through 180°, make a few small stitches in the border to carry the thread to the next horizontal bar, then overcast back again in a similar manner.*

Try to judge renewals of thread in advance so that endings and beginnings occur in the border and not in the work itself, where they are difficult to conceal.

Variations in the ground

◇ In fig. 4, two overcast stitches per bar are shown, but one, three, or four may be used if preferred.

◇ The overcast stitches may be completely upright and very close together. They are then referred to as cording (fig. 5a).

◇ The needle may be carried over the front of the intersections instead of across the back (fig. 5b).

◇ Although the diagonal step-like pathway is traditional for overcasting or cording, some people prefer to work straight across all the horizontal bars, then straight down all the vertical bars (fig. 5c).

◇ Instead of the design being worked first and then the sides of the remaining meshes being overcast, the entire mesh work may be overcast first and the pattern subsequently worked onto it in a running or darning stich.

5a–c *Alternative methods of overcasting the mesh sides.*

FIG. 5a

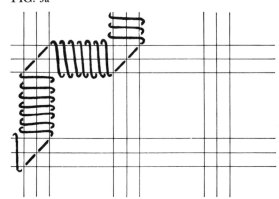

FIG. 5b

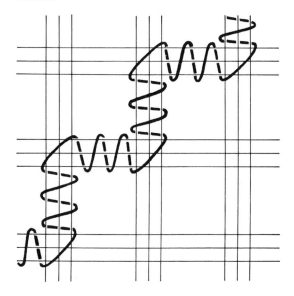

FIG. 5c

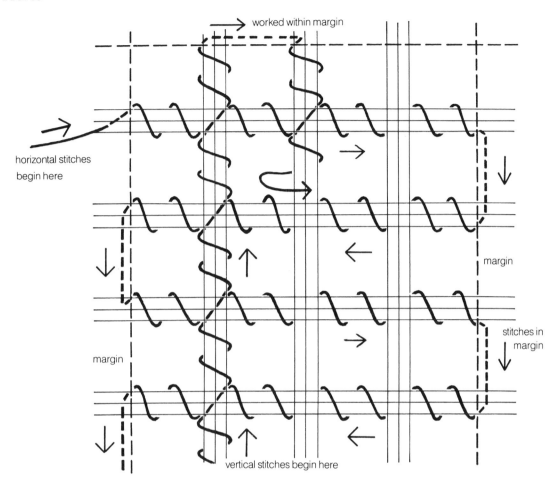

worked within margin

horizontal stitches
begin here

margin

margin

stitches in
margin

vertical stitches begin here

Method 2

Restricted removal of warps and wefts with some cutting.

Parts of the original woven cloth are left untouched to form the design. Only the warps and wefts around this will be taken out to make the square-meshed ground. This involves more work than method 1 since the withdrawn threads have to be cut off at both the margin and the edges of the design, and the cut ends must be fixed so that they cannot fray.

To fix the ends, cut off the warps and wefts a short distance from the design, then either (a)

fold the ends back onto the reverse side and catch them into the cloth with a row of close running stitches (fig. 6a); or (b) thread each cut end one at a time using a sharp-pointed needle and run it back into the margin. If longer ends are left next to the design, the run-in threads will give strength and density to the pattern form.

Alternatively, firm the edges before any cutting of threads is done. Closely oversew, or buttonhole stitch, the entire margin and border of the design. Ease up the threads to be withdrawn, as usual, but snip them off immediately next to the oversewing (fig. 6b).

6 *Fixing the cut ends.*

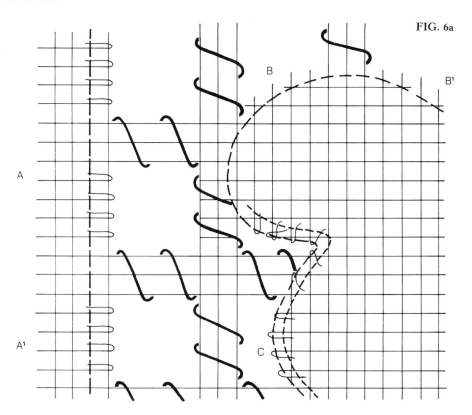

FIG. 6a

6a *In areas A, A¹, eight ends of wefts are cut off, turned back and stitched over. At B, B¹, eight cut ends of warps are not yet turned in. At C, the weft ends are cut off and turned back.*

Method 3

Threads are drawn out in one direction only, that is either the warps or the wefts. This method is sometimes called hemstitching. The removal of wefts in a narrow strip leaves a straight screen of warp threads which can be manipulated with a needle into a variety of patterns. An example is given in fig. 7.

Method 4

Threads are drawn out in one direction only (weft or warp) and are then decorated with needle-weaving. This is sometimes called 'plain weave openwork'. It is particularly associated with Greece, Turkey, Persia, Sicily, China (by introduction), Mexico and South America.

As with method 3, such embroidery is really too heavy, too solid and too restricted in its openwork to be considered a lace, but since it is made with a needle, using a technique found in undoubted needle-made laces, it deserves a mention here.

Use a simple weaving stitch to carry the thread over groups of two, and four, threads alternately as in fig. 8. As the stitches are tightened, the threads are pulled together into columns.

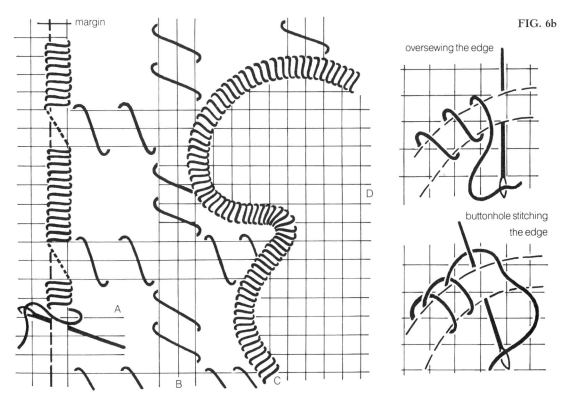

FIG. 6b

oversewing the edge

buttonhole stitching the edge

6b *The edges of the design are oversewn* (**see detail, right**), *and the threads then cut off very closely so that they do not need to be sewn in. A = threads which will be cut hard back when the oversewing of the margin is complete. B = an overcast bar. C = close oversewing around the design. D = the original woven fabric.*

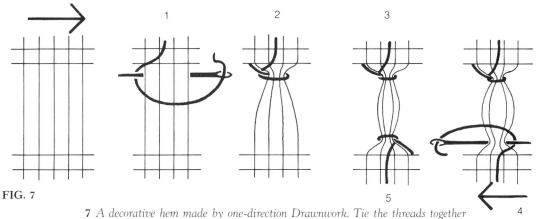

FIG. 7

7 *A decorative hem made by one-direction Drawnwork. Tie the threads together at top and bottom in groups of four. Bring the needle out two threads above the warp strip, pull the thread to the left, pass the needle under the bundle and over the thread as if making a buttonhole stitch. Repeat all along the top border, then all the way back along the bottom border. Splitting the groups on the way back makes for variety.*

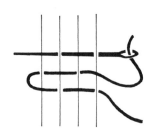

FIG. 8

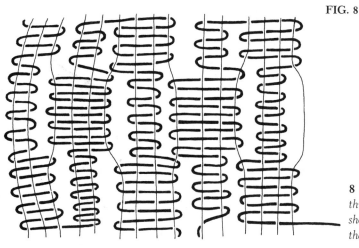

8 *Needleweaving over one-direction threads in regular groupings. The detail shows the over and under movement of the needle.*

Method 5

No threads are drawn out, they are simply pulled together within the fabric. The technique is sometimes known as pulled threadwork, drawn fabric work, or deflected element embroidery. Distinctive types are associated with eighteenth-century Saxony (Dresden work) and the nineteenth-century Philippines where pineapple leaf fibre was used for the base fabric (piña cloth).

FIG. 9a

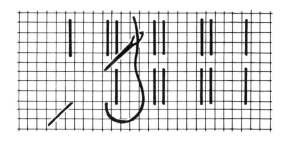

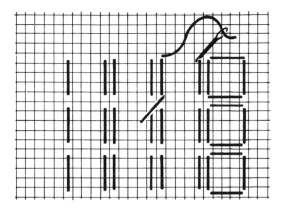

9a–c Three examples of drawn fabric stitches. The squares represent the warps and wefts of the fabric.

9a *Cross filling framed: this is worked in horizontal rows from left to right, and from right to left. Each stitch extends over four threads. All except the outermost are in pairs, which will form the vertical sides of adjacent squares* (above). *The pairs are separated by four threads, where the horizontal sides of each square will be added* (below). (cont. on page 19.)

Opposite Drawnwork from different countries. **Left to right** A stole of piña cloth from the Philippines, worked with tropical fruits in many varied stitches, nineteenth century; peacocks on heavy linen, sixteenth century; a Spanish sampler, *Lo Labro Dona Maria de la Luz, Moreno*, nineteenth century; a Gothic design of putti shooting dragons, worked in red silk on linen, Greek Islands, nineteenth century.

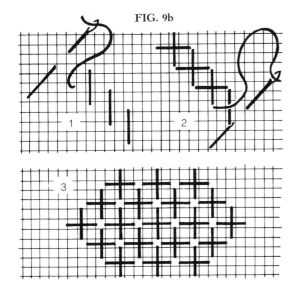

FIG. 9b

Threads are more easily moved in a loosely-woven fabric of fine texture. Most of the stitches used are quite simple. They depend entirely upon the counting of threads and achieve their effect by being pulled tightly so that warps and wefts are drawn apart from their neighbours to form holes. Because of this constant tension, the cloth must be held very firmly in some kind of embroidery frame.

Over fifty varieties of drawn fabric stitches are recorded, but they do not all result in truly openwork effects. Three examples are shown in fig. 9.

9b *Raised band diagonal. (1) Begin at the bottom right-hand corner and work in a vertical direction. Each stitch passes over four threads and is separated by two threads from its neighbour, which is placed four threads up from it. (2) Horizontal stitches are worked on the way back, proceeding downwards from left to right. (3) A detail of the completed work indicating that the more tightly the threads are pulled, the larger the holes will be.*

9c *Diagonal overcast ground with detached eyelet.* **Below left** *The complete work. Begin at A and continue to B, down to C and on towards D. Only three stitches are shown between A and B and the top of each is four threads up and four to the right of its starting point.* **Below right** *The eyelet is worked with eight stitches all radiating from the same hole and extending over four threads measured either vertically or horizontally. Bring the needle out at A and proceed A–O, O–B, B–O, O–C, C–O, O–D, and so on.*

FIG. 9c

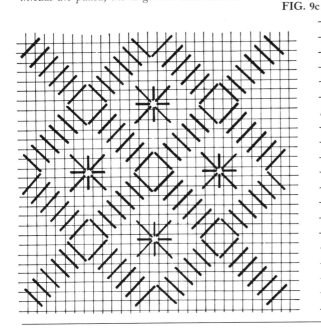

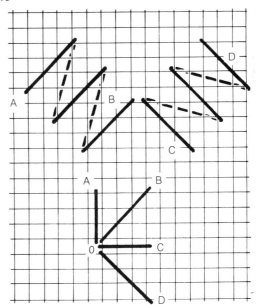

Opposite The varied stitches of Drawnwork, eighteenth century. **Above** Detail of an apron with flounces, cornucopia and butterflies set in woven muslin, Dresden (Saxony). **Below** Drawnwork meshes and pattern surround a pelican piercing its breast to feed its young (Scandinavian).

2
CUTWORK

*C*UTWORK, as used of lace, covers a variety of techniques and appearances. The common factor is the cutting of threads in a woven fabric in order to create a design.

Type 1 Antique Cutwork (also known as Italian Cutwork or *punto tagliato*). Squares are cut out before the main stitching begins. It is an extension of Drawnwork (Chapter 1) and leads on to Reticella and Punto in aria (Chapter 3).

Type 2 The cloth is cut after the main stitching is completed:(a) Richelieu work; (b) Intagliatela or intaglio; (c) Carrickmacross guipure.

Type 3 Holes are cut in the cloth and these holes, rather than the woven fabric, form the design: (a) Broderie anglaise; (b) Ladderwork/Pisa stitch.

Type 4 Ayrshire work. Surface embroidery of the cloth is combined with open areas which contain Drawnwork (Chapter1), buttonhole stitches (Chapters 4-7), or embroidered net (Chapters 11 and 12).

◇DISTRIBUTION Type 1, Antique Cutwork, was made throughout Europe. It was copied in the nineteenth and twentieth centuries in Bologna (Aemilia Ars), in Greece and its islands (Greek lace) and in the English Lake District (Ruskin lace). Types 2 and 4 were made domestically in the nineteenth and twentieth centuries using patterns circulated in the popular ladies' journals or in various DMC (Dolfuss-Meig et Cie) volumes (see Bibliography). Commercially, Carrickmacross was centred in Ireland (see also Chapter 12); Broderie anglaise in Madeira; Ladderwork in Italy, near Florence; and Ayrshire work in western Scotland (Ayr) and northern Ireland.

◇HISTORY Antique Cutwork was used, from at least the fourteenth century, to decorate household and church linens. The first pattern book to mention it (as *ponti tagliato*) was published in 1543 by the Venetian Pagano. From the second half of the sixteenth to the early seventeenth century, Antique Cutwork was very fashionable for ruffs, standing collars and other costume accessories.

Intagliatela dates from the late seventeenth century and represents a cut-price method of producing the effect of an extremely expensive

Venetian gros point (see Chapter 4).

All the remaining types date from the nineteenth century, and most of them continued into the twentieth.

◇MATERIALS   A firmly woven pre-shrunk fabric that will not fray when cut. For type 1, an even-weave is essential, otherwise the squares will turn out to be rectangles.

A needle, slightly blunted, and another more pointed, since some stitches must be made through the fabric as well as around threads.

Sewing threads slightly thicker than the fabric threads and of similar colour; stronger threads for foundation cords.

A support: leather, synthetic leather, glazed linen, waxed cotton, or stiffened card may all be used as a backing. The important thing is that the surface should be hard enough so that the needle glides over it, and not through it. For larger pieces an embroidery frame is helpful; it enables the needle to be taken right through the fabric instead of being stopped by the backing.

Sharp-pointed scissors.

◇STITCHES   Cording, overcasting, needleweaving, detached buttonhole stitching.

Begin with a small and simple pattern; there are plenty of complicated ones to progress to. In each of the types described, the success of the work depends on precision in size, spacing, regularity and tension of the stitches.

Type 1: Antique Cutwork

Setting up the work

The fabric must be constantly under tension. In the sixteenth and seventeenth centuries, it was tacked down to a backing such as parchment; then the parchment was stretched in all directions by cords fixing it to a wooden frame (fig. 10).

Cutting the threads and preparing the spaces

Mark out a 5 cm (2 in) square onto your fabric. This will contain around fifty-four warps and fifty-four wefts, though in the past up to 128 was quite usual. This square will be divided up as shown in fig. 11. Not more that six threads should be left in the areas BCHE and HIJK, and, in the following directions, four are assumed. Overcast all the way round the margin to a sufficient depth to prevent fraying (fig. 12).

To outline the four squares Draw out a single warp immediately next to each of the lines AD, BC, EH and FG. To do this, lift the thread, snip it in the middle, slide it out from between the wefts, and cut it close against the overcast border. Repeat for four single wefts along the lines AF, HJ, IK and DG.

With sharp scissors cut along the narrow gaps

FIG. 10

10 *A sixteenth-century lady referring to a pattern book as she works on a collar stretched in its wooden frame.*

FIG. 11

11 *The squares cut out ready for sewing to begin.*

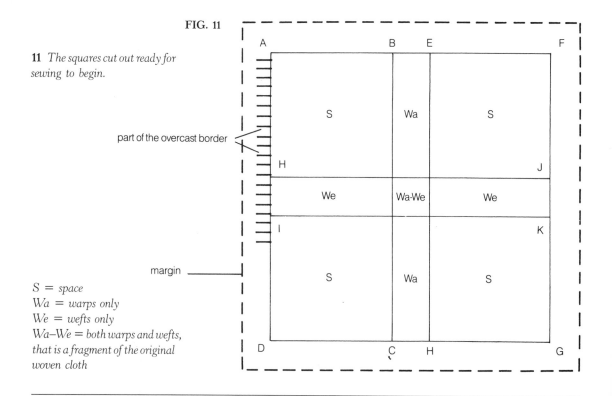

part of the overcast border

margin

S = space
Wa = warps only
We = wefts only
Wa–We = both warps and wefts, that is a fragment of the original woven cloth

FIG. 12

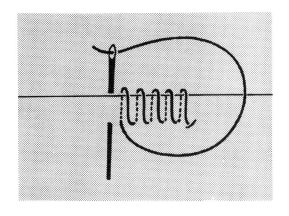

12 *Overcasting stitches worked around the inner borders of the square, using a guide-line to keep the edge straight. This will prevent fraying.*

thus formed, sixteen in all. Trim the threads back to the border. Lift out the central blocks of fabric from each square.

Strengthening the bars

You now have four spaces separated by four bars, each of which consists of four threads. Firm the bars by needleweaving (fig. 13).

Working the design

Work by reference to a drawing or a completed piece, as in a pattern book or sampler.

The overcast borders and the bars between them frame empty spaces, inside which the design will now be added. The spaces are invariably square and the designs restricted to geometric forms (fig. 14).

FIG. 13

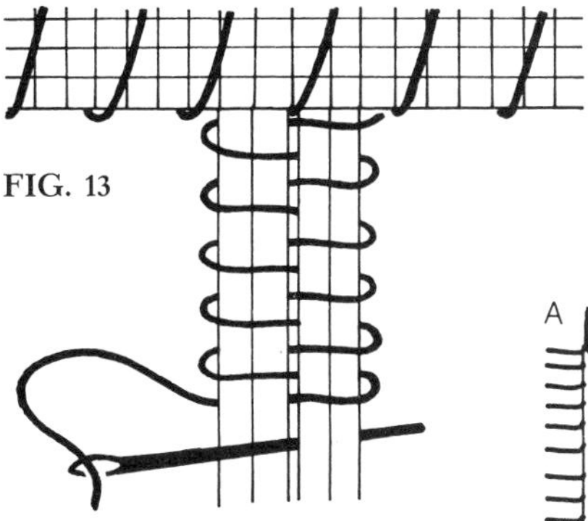

13 *Needleweaving over two pairs of threads. Begin at the outer border, attaching the thread inconspicuously through the overcasting stitches. Take the needle over and under the threads in pairs, pulling the stitches quite tightly.*

FIG. 14

14 *A pattern for Antique Cutwork. This simple design can be used either in isolation, or repeated to form a band, or combined with other designs to make decorative cloths or cushion covers.*
AB = overcast border with cut warps
AH = overcast border with cut wefts

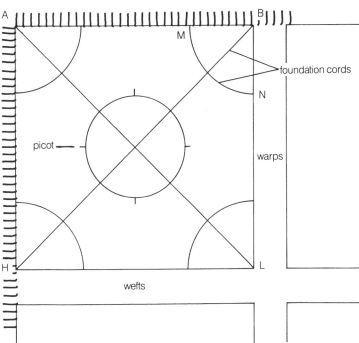

The introduction of foundation cords, also known as foundation strands or supporting strands, marks a new development unknown in Drawnwork. This laying down of threads around which stitches are worked or onto which they are fixed was to become the entire and only skeleton of later needle laces. In Antique Cutwork the object of the cords is to supplement the warp/weft bars by forming diagonals, arcs and circles.

The diagonals Refer to fig. 11 and starting at A, fasten the end of the thread into the reverse side of the overcast border. Take the thread across to the opposite corner, L, pass through the needlewoven bar and return to A. Fix the thread at A, then cover the diagonal with cording (fig. 15). Lay a second double foundation strand between B and H. Cover with cording, as before, but where the two diagonals cross take the thread around the intersection to prevent any displacement.

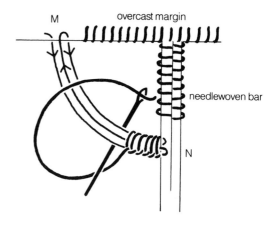

FIG. 16

16 *Buttonholing over the triple foundation cord which forms arc MN. The arrows show the direction of the laying down of the three cords.*

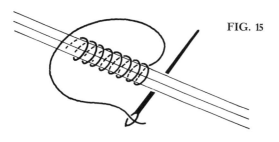

FIG. 15

15 *Cording stitch being worked over a double foundation strand. Cording is similar to the overcasting stitch used in Drawnwork. The stitches are encircling ones, passing round and round two stretched threads and very close together.*

The four arcs Attach a foundation cord to the margin at M. Carry it across to N, leaving it slack so that it forms a curve. Take the thread back to M, and return it to N. Fix it firmly to the bar. Buttonhole stitch along the arc from N to M (fig. 16), with the needle pointing outwards, away from you. Repeat for the other three arcs.

The circle Tie a foundation cord to one of the diagonals with a simple overhand knot (fig. 17). Carry the cord in an arc-like manner to the next diagonal, and take the needle through the cording stitch to catch down the thread. Continue in this way until you have made a circle. Continue around the circle twice more.

FIG. 17

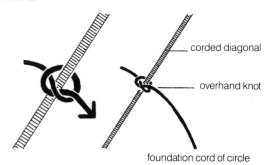

17 *The circle: an overhand knot ties the foundation cord to the diameters.*

18 *Making a bullion stitch picot.*

FIG. 18a

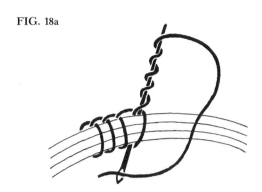

FIG. 18b

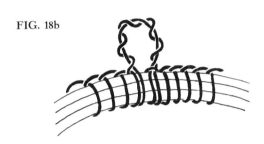

18a *Take the needle part way through the last buttonhole stitch, wind the thread several times around the needle, then pull it through. Go back through the same buttonhole stitch.*
18b *The completed structure.*

Now cover these foundation cords with buttonhole stitches, working with the needle pointing away from the centre. As the mid-point of each segment is reached, add a picot to its outer side (fig. 18). Continue as before until the whole circle is worked. The small square is now completed. Cut through the tacking stitches from the reverse side and release the lace from its backing.

Once these basic procedures are understood it is quite simple to work any lace of this type. Elaborations can be added by: either hemstitching (Chapter 1, page 14), or close buttonhole stitching to make solid areas (Chapter 3, page 39).

Cutwork types 2-4 hover around that grey area where embroidered laces merge into openwork embroideries. They represent an offshoot of what may be regarded as the main line of evolution, in which Cutwork develops into Reticella (Chapter 3) through discarding its base of woven fabric; and on into buttonhole stitch laces (Chapter 4) by constructing each part of the lace – solid design, open ground and decorative fillings – of nothing but multiple variations of the detached buttonhole stitch.

Type 2

Type 2 shows an important feature of later laces which even Reticella does not, namely the division of the lace fabric into (a) a solid area which forms the design, and (b) openwork areas which form the background, or 'ground'. In this type, the design is made of variable shapes of woven cloth, and the ground by bars worked in either buttonhole stitch or cording over supporting strands.

Type 2a: Richelieu work

Whether this technique has any connection with Cardinal Richelieu, advisor to the widowed Anne of Austria during the minority of Louis XIV of France, is speculative. However, antique examples do survive from the seventeenth century, and are known as Intagliatela or Venetian Cutwork (It. *tagliare*, to cut). The designs imitate and often bear a striking resemblance to Venetian needle laces, though the technique is entirely different (see Chapter 4).

As with all Cutwork, a closely-woven cloth is used. Onto this, the pattern (fig. 19a) is printed, transferrred, drawn, or pounced. Traditionally charcoal was tapped through pricked holes in the traced pattern, and the tiny spots joined with ink. Threads do not need to be counted. Tack the fabric to stiff paper, or leather cloth, to provide support.

FIG. 19a

19a *A pattern for Richelieu work.*

FIG. 19b

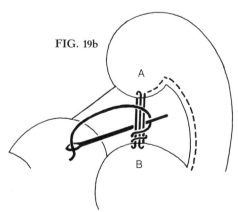

FIG. 19c

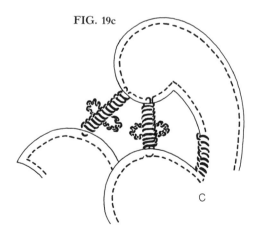

19b *Making the bars of the ground. When the running stitches reach point A, take the thread across to B, back to A, then back again to B. Buttonhole stitch over the three strands from B towards A. At no point must the stitches encircling the bar pass through the underlying fabric. The whole complex of bars must rest above it.*

19c *Two completed bars, with bullion stitch picots. The running stitches have gone right round to C, and the buttonholing of the outer border of the design has begun.*

FIG. 20

20 *A twentieth-century Richelieu work design. The small circles on the bars represent bullion stitch picots and the short straight lines, Venetian picots.*

Outlining the pattern

Outline the pattern in running stitches. Each time a bar position is reached, make a three-strand foundation cord (fig. 19b). Work bullion stitch picots (fig. 18) where these are indicated on the pattern. Complete the running stitches of the entire outline, and the buttonhole stitching of all the bars. Now buttonhole stitch around all parts of the design, covering the running stitches, and working very closely and firmly so that when the fabric is finally cut away the ends will not pull from the stitches and fray (fig. 19c).

The central decorations of the flowers may be added by Drawnwork (Chapter 1, method 5, page 16) or by surface embroidery.

Creating the openwork

Once the design is complete, it is time to create the openwork. Turn to the reverse side and cut through the tacking stitches which hold the cloth to its support. Then, using a pair of sharply-pointed scissors and extreme care, cut around the whole design, close to the buttonhole stitching and passing under all the bars so that they are not damaged. Remove the surplus cloth. The photograph on page 35 shows the dramatic effect of the heavy design and bar-traversed spaces.

Fig. 19a. is based on an antique design but the technique can be applied equally well to modern forms (fig. 20).

Type 2b: Intagliatela

Intagliatela is worked in the same way as Richelieu work. In addition, to give the raised effect of a Venetian gros point, the outlines of the flowers are thickly padded with coarse strands of thread cut to different lengths so that the final shaping is smoothly graded (fig. 21). Cover this padding with close buttonhole stitching.

FIG. 21

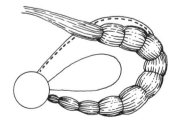

21 *The padding strands making a raised outline in Intagliatela.*

Type 2c: Carrickmacross guipure

This has a similar, though not identical technique to type 2b. The fabric is not a thick cotton or linen, but a translucent batiste; the pattern is printed or drawn not on the fabric itself but on a pattern tacked beneath it; and the designs are outlined not with buttonhole stitches, but with a couched cord. The term 'guipure' refers to the bars by which the cloth design areas are linked together (see also Chapter 12).

Type 3

Here there is no structured or worked ground. The lace consists simply of the woven fabric and the holes made in it, which form the design. This is a lace only when the openwork is sufficiently extensive. It is of significance in providing a link, technically, via Ladderwork, between Antique Cutwork and Richelieu work.

Type 3a: Broderie anglaise
MADEIRA WORK, EYELET WORK

The base fabric is a firmly woven cotton and the embroidery thread is white or, in Madeira work, a pale sea-green. The eyelet holes are round or oval.

The positions of the eyelet holes are marked on the fabric by printing or transferring, and then each is outlined in running stitches. The centre of the eyelet is cut out with sharp-pointed scissors (fig. 22). Where the holes are too small for scissors, they can be pierced with a stiletto or awl.(In the nineteenth century, it was possible to buy lengths of cloth with the holes for this work already punched.) Overcast the raw edges so that the running stitches are completely covered. Alternatively, turn the edge under before overcasting.

Padding is occasionally added along the lower

FIG. 22

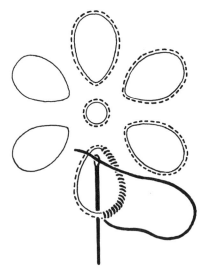

22 *Outlining the eyelet holes with running stitch, in Broderie anglaise. Both the raw edge and the running stitches are overcast.*

FIG. 23

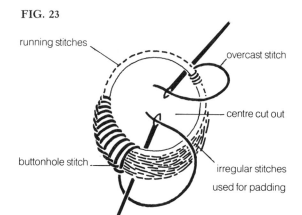

running stitches

overcast stitch

centre cut out

buttonhole stitch

irregular stitches used for padding

23 *Padding the lower border of a Broderie anglaise eyelet.*

border of selected holes to give them greater prominence: numerous irregular stitches provide bulk, which is then buttonhole stitched over while the unpadded upper border is overcast (fig. 23). A similar technique is used for the scalloped lower edge of Broderie anglaise flounces (fig. 24).

FIG. 24

scalloped border

24 *Detail of a Broderie anglaise flounce showing the pattern made by openwork, not by solid areas.*

Type 3b: Venetian ladderwork

ANGLAISE À BARRETTES, FRENCH CUTWORK, PISA STITCH

This represents a transition from a design made by holes to a design outlined by holes. An extension of the surrounding openwork, and the introduction of more bars, would produce Richelieu work.

The larger holes characteristic of this type make it necessary for their sides to be held together by bars to maintain their shape. A sixteenth-century form is shown in fig. 25 a and b. Here, the bars are tightened so that the work has something of the appearance of a string of irregular sausages. In the nineteenth and twentieth centuries (fig. 25c) the bars were frequent, straight and untensioned like the rungs of a ladder, hence

25a–c *Ladderwork.*

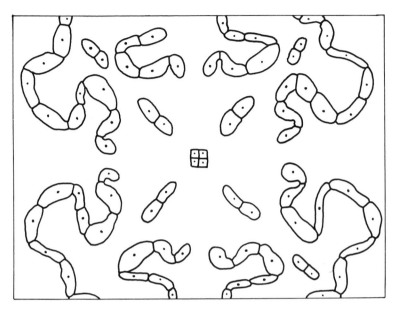

FIG. 25a

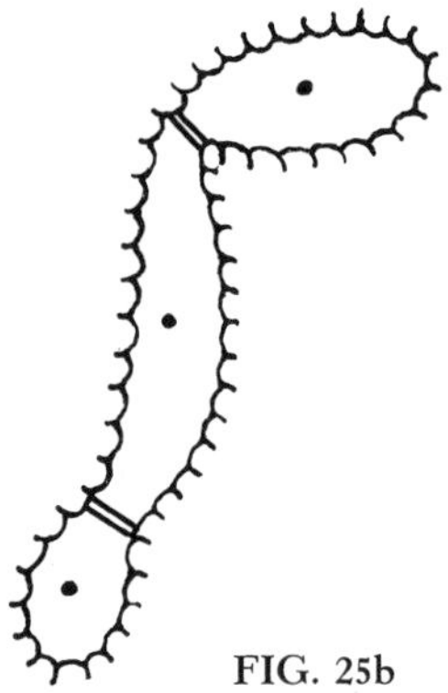

FIG. 25b

25a *The bars are pulled tight, giving the long holes a segmented appearance, c.1600.*
25b *Detail of (a) showing the tightened oversewing which produces a crenellated edge to the turned-under fabric.*

the names 'ladderwork' and 'Broderie anglaise with bars'.

The method for working is similar to Richelieu work. In nineteenth-century instructions the cloth with its imprinted design was supported by 'moleskin', which probably referred to a double-twill fustian, though very soft leather was sometimes used.

Once the running stitches and the bars have been completed, there are two alternatives:

(a) The unwanted fabric is cut away, leaving a narrow margin around the running stitches, and the bars intact. The raw edge is turned under as the outline is overcast (see type 3a).

(b) The overcasting is worked first and the cutting done afterwards (see type 2a).

Type 4: Ayrshire work

This is basically a white surface embroidery using satin stitch and some stem stitch. Apart from occasional eyelet holes, the openwork is restricted to the flower centres or other small decorative areas. The types of fillings used relate Ayrshire work technically to lace in the following ways:

(a) Drawnwork, with any of its fifty varied stitches (see Chapter 1, method 5, page 16).

(b) The centres are cut out, then filled with:

(i) any of the forty or so fancy buttonhole stitches mentioned in Chapter 4;

(ii) machine net. Two-twist bobbinet is stitched over the holes from the reverse side and is decorated with a selection of the fifty-plus run stitches referred to in Chapters 11 and 12.

FIG. 25c

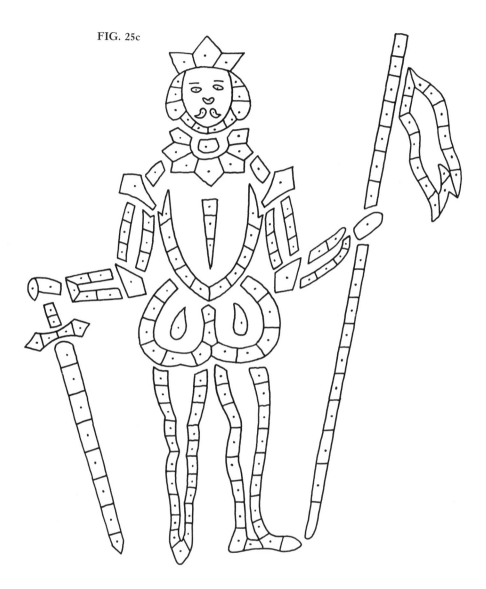

25c *A modern design: a knight outlined with extensive ladderwork. The areas to be cut out are marked with dots.*

3
RETICELLA

ALL THE examples described in Chapters 1 and 2 are embroidered laces. That is, they begin with a woven fabric and by displacing, pulling out, or cutting threads, create in that solid mass an openwork or lace. Reticella represents a very important move away from the Drawnwork and Cutwork techniques. Although it often uses precisely the same patterns and stitches as Antique Cutwork, the stitches are not made in a woven fabric base. They have to be made purely out of the movements of the needle and thread around each other 'in the air'. This concept is rendered by the Italian term *punto in aria* which means, literally, 'stitches in the air'.

To make the lace, a scaffolding of foundation cords is constructed in the form of squares, diagonals, arcs or triangles. Solid areas of design enclosed by these cords are filled with one predominant stitch, the buttonhole stitch. However, since all the hundreds of so-called needle or needlepoint laces are made in this way (see especially Chapters 4 and 5), distinctions between them are necessary, and the name Reticella was chosen for what might be regarded as imitation or substitute Antique Cutwork. The word means 'net-cell' (It. *rete-cella*), or 'little net', and refers to the square shapes which contain the design.

'Reticella' first appeared in a pattern book by Passarotti printed in Bologna in 1591, where it was referred to by its adjectival form *punto reticello*. At that time, however, it was also described as 'Cutwork'— an obvious misnomer since there were no pre-existing threads to be cut. Nevertheless the use of the term is clearly indicated in fig. 26, taken from Vinciolo's pattern book of 1606, where he calls both Reticella and Cutwork 'ouvrages de point couppe'. The practice, though confusing to us, was probably a commercial manoeuvre. Reticella could be made more quickly and less expensively than Cutwork, therefore selling it under that name could increase the merchants' profits. Its technique also had the advantage over Cutwork in that, instead of being made inside the cloth which it decorates so that it could not later be moved, it was made as a separate piece and so could be transferred as desired from one garment to another.

◇DISTRIBUTION   Seventeenth-century Reticella was associated with Italy and France and, later, Greece, in fact probably most areas where Antique Cutwork was also made. Thus the blanket usage of 'Cutwork' makes it very

Ouurages de point couppe.

FIG. 26

26 *A Vinciolo pattern for lace to decorate a ruff.*
Below *Cutwork surrounded by dotted lines which indicate Drawnwork and the fact that the lace is made within a fabric.*
Centre *Reticella – the simple lines around the squares represent foundation cords, indicating that no woven fabric was involved in its manufacture.*
Above *Punto in aria built around curved foundation cords.*

difficult to know from historical records which of the two techniques is intended.

◇HISTORY Reticella began after Cutwork, but both were used for fashion during the period when fine square-framed openworks were in enormous demand for the decoration of ruffs, cuffs and coifs.

◇MATERIALS A pattern (fig. 29, page 38).

Strong thread for the foundation cords; sewing thread, preferably linen, firmly twisted.

A blunt-tipped needle for working the stitches, and a pointed needle for tacking the pattern down in the initial stages.

As there is no woven fabric to be stretched, an embroidery frame is not needed. Several folds of cloth, a parchment, or a small hard cushion, can be used as support. The work must lie flat.

◇STITCHES Needleweaving or plaiting, for strands to make the outlines of the square frames as alternatives to a simple foundation cord; buttonhole stitches for the design.

Constructing the skeleton

Reticella by-passes all the drawing out and cutting off of warps and wefts, all the oversewing of the inner borders to prevent fraying, and all the resultant wastage of the pieces of cloth that are removed. Its construction begins at stage four of Antique Cutwork, working the design (page 23). The outer border (AFGD) and the lines of warps (BEHC) and wefts (HIKJ) (fig. 11, page 22), are replaced by pre-made plaited or needlewoven strands, or by foundation cords not unlike those used to make the diagonals, arcs

and circles of fig. 14, page 23. Fig. 27 on page 37 shows the features which distinguish completed Cutwork from completed Reticella.

Reticella can be worked over a pattern, unlike Antique Cutwork which needs the guidance of a book. Traditionally the pattern was drawn in ink on parchment. In the early twentieth century it was printed in white or silver on black paper (fig. 28, page 37) to make the foundation cords stand out clearly. Today, tracings of patterns can be made onto architect's linen, and backed with a dark fabric which acts as a support.

Opposite Cutwork. **Back left to right** Antique Cutwork: an early seventeenth-century linen cloth, the large squares filled with geometric designs of triangles, arcs and circles, some of Reticella construction; the border is plaited bobbin lace. Richelieu work: bold flowers and leaves linked by bars; the intervening cloth areas are cut away, leaving an openwork (nineteenth century). Ruskin work: a cushion cover worked in the Antique Cutwork manner, showing strips of Cutwork separated by narrow bands of Drawnwork. **Below right** 'Modern Greek embroidery', nineteenth century. **Below centre** Modern Greek embroidery, Cyprus, 1985.

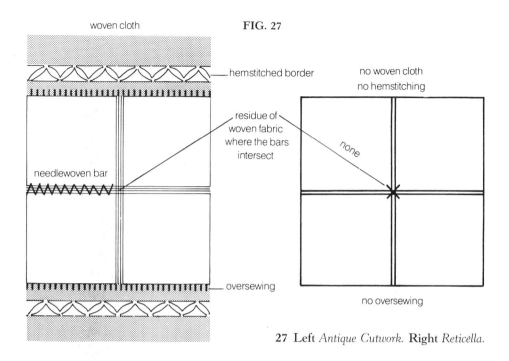

woven cloth   **FIG. 27**

hemstitched border

no woven cloth
no hemstitching

residue of
woven fabric
where the bars
intersect

needlewoven bar

oversewing

no oversewing

27 Left *Antique Cutwork.* **Right** *Reticella.*

FIG. 28

28 *A pattern for Reticella printed in white on black paper, early twentieth century.*

Opposite Cutwork – the holes form the design. **Above left to right** A transfer pattern for a ladderwork collar, the dots indicate areas to be cut out; Broiderie anglaise partly worked; a punched pattern for a pair of cuffs. **Below** A baby cap in Ayrshire work, the cut-out areas filled with varied buttonhole stitches; a Madeira work pattern for a baby's bodice, and the finished embroidery.

Attach the pattern shown in fig. 29 to a support. Prick small holes, between 2 mm ($\frac{1}{16}$ in) and 4 mm ($\frac{2}{16}$) apart, on either side of every line of the pattern and at every intersection (fig. 30a), but omitting the diagonals in the first and last squares.

Apply two foundation cords along each outline. Couch down the cords by passing the needle through the holes already made (fig. 30b). These same stitches can be used to attach the work to the support, or tacking stitches can be used after the pricking and couching has been completed. For internal lines, use a single foundation cord held down in a similar manner, unless some emphasis is required, when two or more cords may be used.

Working the design

The pattern, with the exception of the four triangles marked X in the two centre squares, is made as for Cutwork (page 24), but any stitches attached to the outer frames will be hitched over the foundation cord instead of through overcasting stitches (fig. 31). These outer frames are often left uncovered so that they are ready for insertion, or joining to other pieces. If desired, however, they may be overcast, corded or buttonhole-stitched with the needle pointing outwards. Bullion stitch picots can be added to the outer borders of the arcs or circles (see page 25).

29 *A pattern for Reticella.*

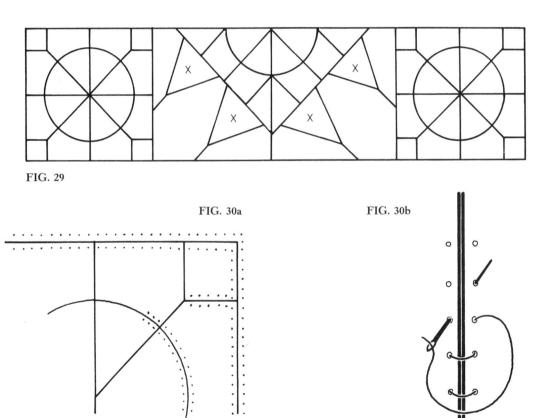

FIG. 29

FIG. 30a

FIG. 30b

30a *Pricking the pattern.*
30b *Couching over a double strand of foundation cords, using the pricked holes.*

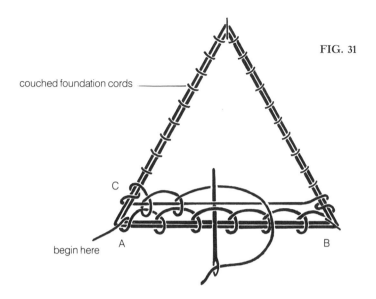

FIG. 31

couched foundation cords

C

begin here   A   B

31 *Filling in the triangle. Work the first row of detached buttonhole stitches from left to right (A to B) over the foundation cord. The loops between the stitches should be left slack. It is not easy, at first, to keep an even tension. At B, take the thread twice around the foundation cord, then carry it straight back to the left side. At C, twist it twice around the foundation cord. Work buttonhole stitches back to the right-hand side, taking in both the return thread and the loops of the previous row. Every stitch must be of the same size and shape as in the first row. Continue in this way until the triangle is filled, reducing the number of stitches per row as you work towards the apex.*

    Note: *All thread ends should be left at the sides of the triangles. Before starting any row, check that the thread is long enough to get you to the end.*

The four triangles

These will be solidly filled with a form of buttonhole stitch used in almost every type of needle lace. This widely-occurring stitch is the 'detached buttonhole stitch with a straight return' (see Chapter 4, page 46). It can be worked either closely together (close form) or spaced apart (open form). Refer to fig. 31 for working instructions. This shows the stitch in its 'open' form, but traditionally the stitches are packed very closely together. Once you have mastered the technique, proceed to the 'close' form.

When working the triangle, the lace has to be handled a lot, and the threads must sometimes be pressed down with the thumb to firm the stitches. To protect the lace from this excessive contact you can use a plastic shield with a sufficiently large window cut in it to allow all the necessary needle movements. As you go from one triangle to another, take the window with you.

To release the lace
Cut through the stitches which hold pattern and support together, from the reverse side. If a

double layer of cloth has been used as a backing, it is easier to cut the stitches between the two layers. Also from the reverse side, cut through the couching stitches which hold the foundation cords to the pattern. Lift off the lace. Any thread ends can now be fastened off at the back.

Variations

Braided and needlewoven strands

In the sixteenth- and seventeenth-century Reticellas, strands made by plaiting or needleweaving together four threads were used in place of foundation cords for outlining the squares, and sometimes for the diagonals. This is a very distinctive feature, and provides an interesting example of a lace made by a mixture of two techniques, since the long threads required for plaiting would probably have been wound on bobbins to prevent them tangling.

Aemilia Ars lace

The Aemilia Ars Society was founded in Bologna in 1898 for the resurrection of antique crafts of various kinds. The Society foundered on internal dissent in 1903, but continued to make lace both for exhibition and tourist purposes until the late

FIG. 32

32 *A Passarotti design for the Orsini Malvezzi heraldic emblems. This was copied by the Aemilia Ars Society. The little spikes on some of the stems and leaves indicate picots.*

1920s and won a number of gold medals. The lace mainly copied was *punto di reticello*, or Reticella, as described in this chapter. Some of their best-known pieces were their copies of the series of decorative coats of arms designed by Arcangelo Passarotti in 1591 for the noble ladies of Bologna who were his patrons (fig. 32).

In fig. 32, the Reticella technique can be clearly identified by the lack of any hemstitching around the lace. The straight lines are the foundation cords dividing the area into traditional squares; but for Passarotti these were no more than a trelliswork to which the boldly curving stems of fruits and flowers could cling. Unconfined now by warp and weft, the pattern bursts from its frame, shaking off the restricting geometric triangles, arcs and circles to become exuberantly free and lively. This step was of the utmost importance in the development of later needle laces. The solid areas of the design are filled with close buttonhole stitching.

Another Passarotti innovation was the introduction of raised decoration, which was rare in the sixteenth century. The dots over the upper and lower fronds in fig. 32 indicate surface picots. These are very similar in construction to bullion stitch picots (fig. 18, page 25), but they are attached to the front of the solid buttonhole stitching in such a way that they stand upright like a small spike, arch over in a loop, or lie flat.

To make a picot in relief Fig. 33a. Bring the needle out at A. Make a very small stitch into the close buttonhole stitching of the design area, and bring the needle out again at A. Twist the thread ten or twelve times around the needle as shown. Draw the needle carefully through the twists, holding these down with the thumb. This will give an arched picot. If it is made in isolation, fasten off the thread at the back of the work.

To make a flat picot Fig. 33b. Proceed as for the arched, but instead of pulling the thread tightly back to A, leave it stretched out and take the needle down at B. Emerge at A[1] and work a second picot between A[1] and B[1].

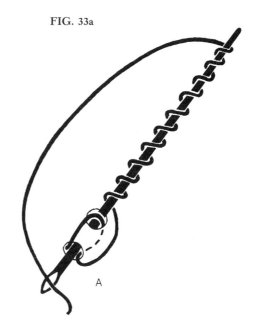

FIG. 33a

33a *The arched picot.*

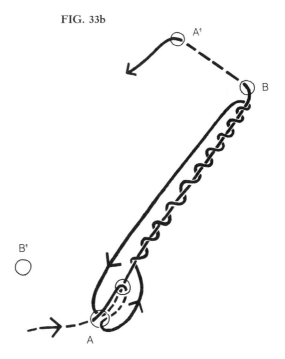

FIG. 33b

33b *The flat picot. The arrows indicate the sequence of thread movements.*

FIG. 34a   **FIG. 34b**

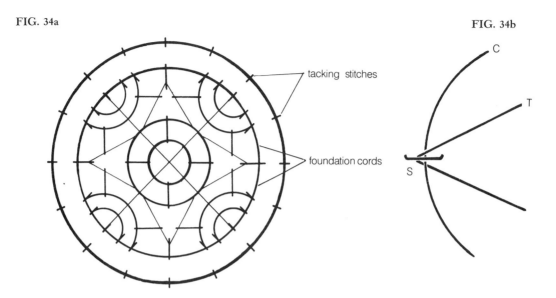

tacking stitches

foundation cords

34a *An Aemilia Ars pattern. The heavy lines represent support stitches through which the foundation cords are threaded. Tacking stitches hold the pattern to the underlying support cloth.*

34b *Detail of a supporting loop (S) holding the foundation cord for the triangle (T) and the circle (C). This is an alternative to their being held down by couching.*

The Aemilia Ars Society often used circular instead of square shapes for isolated motifs intended to be inserted into, or applied onto, cloth. These latter forms were known as incrustations. The lacemakers of the Society, according to some accounts, did not couch down the foundation cords. Instead they looped them through specially constructed support stitches (fig. 34). The advantage of this method over the normal Reticella one is doubtful. The outer borders of the design areas in Aemilia Ars laces were commonly buttonhole-stitched to give them emphasis. This was not usual in antique Reticellas or Cutworks.

Punto in aria

The makers of Reticella imposed on themselves the same discipline as the makers of Antique Cutwork, that is they restricted the design within square frames, simply replacing the warps and

wefts of a woven fabric by foundation cords laid freely over a pattern.

It is clear from Vinciolo's ruff design (fig. 26) that, though it might be commercially advantageous to imitate the popular Cutwork in this manner, it was early realized that the foundation cords did not have to lie straight, but could be made to curve. Thus the outer border shows layers of piled-up loops – made initially of gold thread to enhance the inner white linen. Such loops were known as *purling*.

To make the purling, lay down curved foundation cords, buttonhole stitch over them and add picots, exactly in the manner of branching bars (fig. 35).

From this rigid purling, it was a short but imaginative step to designs such as the elaborate heraldic birds at the top of the Passarotti woodcut (fig. 32).

Purling, the birds, and indeed all later button-

FIG. 35

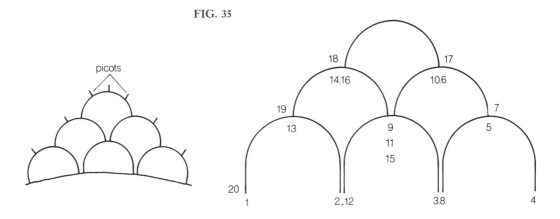

hole-stitch laces are, technically, forms of Punto in aria: their stitches are made 'in the air', that is not *inside* a fabric but *over* a pattern. Such an extremely broad usage is almost meaningless. It requires subdivision: into Reticella, Venetian, English and other localised needle laces, all of which developed their own distinctive features.

Thus 'Punto in aria' has lost its general significance and is used only as a specific term for laces of the late sixteenth/early seventeenth centuries which were geometrically curved or toothed, and which formed the outer free borders of Reticella or Antique Cutwork decorations. More rarely, it was used of larger pieces of the same period which did not have a specific locale.

In succeeding decades a fierce competition developed between the various centres of lace production. Each began to specialize in a particular technique, and the older broad terms –

35 *Purling as it appears in Vinciolo's pattern (fig. 26). Work in the following sequence. By so doing, the whole course can be covered by a continuous thread without joins.*

1 – 2 – 3 – 4	*lay foundation strand (s)*
4 – 5	*buttonhole stitch over (b)*
5 – 6	*s*
6 – 7 – 8 – 9	*b*
9 – 10	*s*
10 – 11 – 12 – 13	*b*
13 – 14 – 15	*s*
15 – 16	*b*
16 – 17	*s*
17 – 18 – 19 – 20	*b*

Drawnwork, Cutwork, Reticella, Punto in aria – were dropped in favour of names which promoted commercially the place of origin of the lace rather than describing, in a general way, their method of manufacture.

4
VENETIAN LACE

VENICE was the first centre of lace production to emerge from the general geometric Punto in aria form and to create designs and techniques which were entirely its own. The basic method of manufacture – laying down foundation strands and infilling the solid parts of the design with buttonhole stitches – remained the same, but the high padded outlines, the variety of decorative fillings and the beautiful arrangements of ornamental bars forming a structured ground, distinguished Venice in the seventeenth century from any other centre of production and fully justified the name 'Venetian lace'.

◇DISTRIBUTION

Today, 'Venetian lace' covers many derivative forms, but initially the lace was peculiar to the Venetian Republic. The precise location of the professional manufactories is uncertain, and some may have been at the convent on the tiny fishing island of Burano, five miles beyond the city. Venetian lace was copied in France, from 1665 to around 1700. In the late nineteenth and early twentieth centuries copies of varying faithfulness were made in Belgium (point de Venise), Burano, Bayeux (point Colbert), Vienna, Ireland (Inishmacsaint and Kenmare), and the Barcelona area of Spain.

◇HISTORY

The production of the distinctive Venetian laces began about 1650 and ended around 1700, when deterioration and flattening had already affected them for some time.

◇MATERIALS

In the seventeenth century, extremely fine linen thread was used, (almost ten times finer than anything available 300 years later) and densities of over 6,000 buttonhole stitches to the square inch were obtained. It is recommended that newcomers begin with thickish thread. This makes it easier to master the techniques and to see where, if anywhere, you have gone wrong.

A slightly blunted needle for making the stitches, and a pointed needle for other work.

Also, a drawn or printed pattern; a pricking needle; foundation cord; supporting cloth; thin plastic to cover the pattern; and coarse strands of thread for padding the raised outline (cordonnet). Woodcuts from eighteenth-century Venice indicate that the lace was made on a pillow or cushion. Elsewhere, probably only parchment was used.

◇STITCHES It is the exclusive use of buttonhole stitches which characterizes true needle, or needlepoint, laces – as distinct from the term 'needle-made', which covers all laces made with a sewing needle. The detached buttonhole stitch with a straight return, close form, is used uniquely for the solid parts of the design. The decorative fillings, however, can use forty or more varieties of buttonhole stitch. Couching stitches, which are later removed, are used to hold down the foundation cords.

FIG. 36

36 *Pattern for Belgian point de Venise: white outlines on black paper.*

FIG. 37

37 *The same pattern, black on white, indicating the areas to be filled by different stitches.*

The pattern

The example of Belgian point de Venise shown in fig.36, though updated from the seventeenth-century form, gives some idea of the flowing curvaceous stems and rounded flowers of the antique style. It differs from seventeenth-century Venetian laces in its flattened form, simplified design, coarser thread and spaced out stitches.

In the past, patterns were drawn in black ink on green-tinted parchment. Today, a white outline on black card combines firmness of support with clarity of line and the contrasting shade shows up the sewing threads. Tracings can, alternatively, be made on to architect's linen, which is then backed by stiffened cloth for ease of handling, and covered with thin plastic to protect the lace from contact with the ink. Use fig. 37 as your pattern.

The outline or scaffolding

Once the pattern is set up, foundation cords can be laid down. These act as a sort of clothes line on which the loops of the buttonhole stitches will be hung. The cords along the sides provide anchors so that the drag and tension of successive rows of stitches do not distort the shape and cause the work to sag.

To lay the cords Proceed as in Reticella (Chapter 3, page 38). Use a sharp needle mounted in a wooden handle to prick small pairs of holes at frequent intervals along the inked lines, every 2 mm ($\frac{1}{16}$ in) to 4 mm ($\frac{2}{16}$ in). Then stretch the foundation cord gradually along every part of the outline between the pairs of holes, fixing it down with couching stitches as shown in fig. 30b, page 38.

Filling in the solid parts of the design

The lace now presents the appearance of blank shapes waiting to be filled in – like those in a child's colouring book. Instead of varying colours, however, types of stitches are used.

Area 1 The more solid parts are to be filled using the detached buttonhole stitch with a straight return. This stitch, which has already appeared in Reticella (Chapter 3, pages 32-43), is a constant factor in all needle/needlepoint laces with the exception of those made in England (Chapter 5) and Hungary (Chapter 6). In its close form it appears in Venetian, Burano and French (Alençon and Argentan) laces; in its open form in Belgian laces such as point de Venise and Point de gaze.

The decorative fillings

Variations of the detached buttonhole stitch are used to provide lightness and decoration to selected areas. To fill in the areas marked (2), (3) and (4), refer to figs. 38-40.

Working the structured ground

Venetian lace was distinguished from the earlier Punto in aria by: (a) the foundation cords curving freely to form a wide variety of plant and animal shapes instead of being restricted to geometric arcs, triangles, squares and circles; and (b)the parts of the lace being clearly separated into solid design and openwork ground areas. Such a ground was not an entirely new concept, having been foreshadowed in the earlier Drawnworks (Chapter 1, page 8), but it was new to needle laces, and a Venetian innovation. The new grounds were 'structured'; that is, they consisted of special thread arrangements intended to link the solid design areas together and to hold them in place.

In fig. 36, the ground is made by straight bars. These are added after the design areas are completed. Lightweight bars are made over a single supporting strand of thread, heavier bars over three strands. Attach one end of the thread to the foundation cord of the design. Carry it across the space to another part of the design. Using the same thread, buttonhole stitch over the bar cord until you are back at the starting point. Take the thread around the foundation cord of the design until the next bar position is reached. Repeat this procedure in every place where bars

38 *Area 2: Begin at the left side of the base of the flower centre, throwing the first row of stitches over the foundation cord. Work the stitches in pairs, leaving longer loops between the pairs. At the right-hand side, coil the thread around the cord twice. Work back to the left-hand side, again with paired stitches alternating with those of the previous row. Continue until the space is filled. All thread ends must be left at the foundation cords to be tidied later so that there are no joins in the middle of the work. These will be worked in later.*

39 *Area 3: Detached buttonhole stitch is worked fairly loosely to and fro, left to right and right to left, in a horizontal direction.*

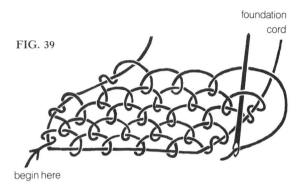

FIG. 39

foundation cord

begin here

FIG. 38

foundation cord

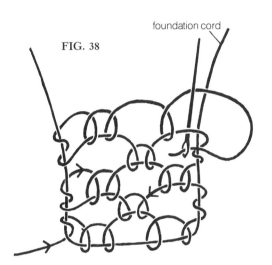

40 *Area 4: This is worked in the same way as area (1), but on the third row small holes are created at intervals by missing two loops, then taking the thread fairly slackly across the gap before continuing. Row 4, carry the thread straight back from left to right. Row 5, make three stitches over the three floating threads, replacing the loops missed out.*

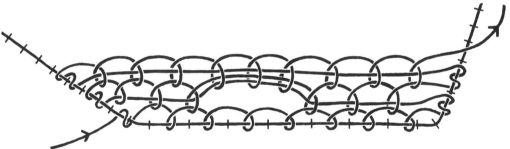

FIG. 40

are indicated. To make a three-strand bar support, work as shown in fig. 20a, but continue from one bar to the next as for the single strand.

Branching bars In four places in fig. 36 the bars branch. Ideally the same thread should be used, in complete continuity. Refer to fig. 41 for working instructions. Where the branching is slightly more extensive, the cord is moved back

and forth in an almost maze-like manner (see Chapter 3, purling, page 43 and Chapter 7, page 80). Where the branching ground is very extensive (as it often is in Belgian point de Venise, the Irish Youghal lace and the seventeenth-century point de France), so that the appearance is less that of bars than of overgrown meshes, additional support and guidance is needed if a very regular

FIG. 41

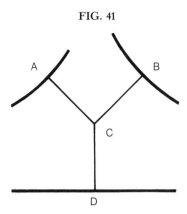

FIG. 42a

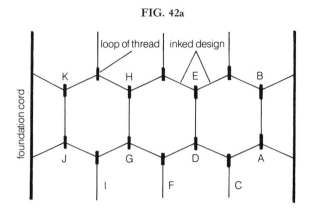

FIG. 42b

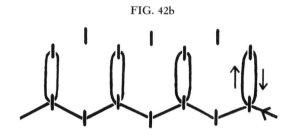

FIG. 42c

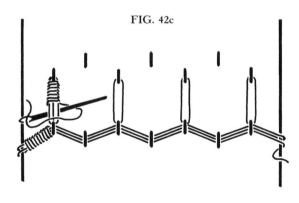

FIG. 43

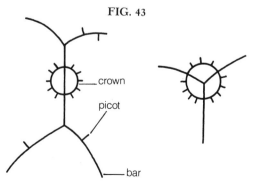

41 *The order for oversewing branching bars. Take the foundation cord slackly from A to B. Buttonhole stitch from B to C. Take the cord from C to D. Buttonhole stitch from D to C, and from C to A.*

42 *Working an extensive branching ground.*
42a *The inked pattern outlining a meshwork of bars. Loops of thread have been added at every line junction to act as guides for the laying of the foundation cords (a method similar to that used by the Aemilia Ars Society for Reticella).*
42b *Threading the supporting strands through the loops. These strands will outline the large meshes. Attach the sewing thread to the nearest foundation cord. Pass the needle through the loops in the order: AB, BA, AC, CD, DE, ED, DF, FG, GH, HG etc, to J. Twist the thread around the foundation cord next to J. This will give single strands along the bottom of the meshes, and double along the sides. Bring the cord back through the row of loops from J to A; around the foundation cord; back again from A to J; ending at the foundation cord beyond.*
42c *Buttonhole stitch over the triple strands to bring the needle from the foundation cord to J. Take the thread up to K. Buttonhole stitch from K to J, then J to I and I to G. Take the thread up to H; buttonhole stitch from H to G, G to F, F to D. Continue in this manner to complete the first row. Repeat the sequence in all sub-sequent rows. When the gound is complete, every side of every mesh will be covered with buttonhole stitches.*

43 *The starry decorations of seventeenth-century Venetian gros point ground.*

appearance is required (fig. 42). Such grounds are much too extensive to be worked in one continuous thread. Endings and beginnings of thread should be made only at the foundation cords, with small knots which will be concealed later by additional outlining threads.

Bars with crowns In seventeenth-century Venetian laces the bars were short and ornamented with delicate half-wheels and circles, each radiating tiny picot-spikes (fig. 43). Two such 'crowns' are indicated at the left of fig. 36. The picots were sometimes bullion stitch (see fig. 44b), or buttonhole stitched, or made in the manner of minute purling (see fig. 35, page 43).

Raising the outline

The best Venetian laces were raised, that is they had additional outlines added over the foundation cords of the design. These additions were often padded to an enormous extent, rising 2.5 mm ($\frac{1}{10}$ in) or more above the lace surface. The padding consists of thick strands of linen tow, tapered at either end to shape the central bulge. It is couched over the foundation cord where needed, then covered with extremely close buttonhole stitching (fig. 44a). Protruding from this are separately attached clusters of little bullion stitch picots, and crowns of great variety (fig. 44b).

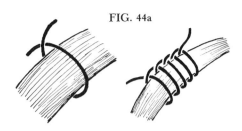

FIG. 44a

44a *The appearance of buttonhole stitches over padding strands.*

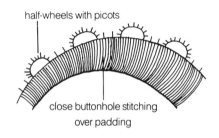

half-wheels with picots

close buttonhole stitching over padding

FIG. 44b

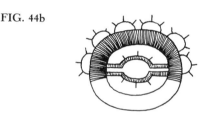

44b *Two examples of three-dimensional raising in seventeenth-century Venetian gros point.*

FIG. 45

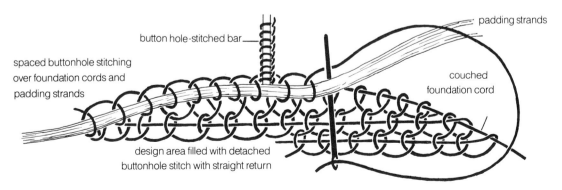

button hole-stitched bar

spaced buttonhole stitching over foundation cords and padding strands

padding strands

couched foundation cord

design area filled with detached buttonhole stitch with straight return

45 *Belgian point de Venise: attaching the cordonnet over the foundation cords with spaced buttonhole stitching.*

In later Venetian lace derivatives this impressive sculpturing, sometimes likened to carved ivory, was reduced to one or more strands of outlining cord, which gave definition to the design but barely took it into the third dimension. Such strands, still known as cordonnets, were fixed to the lace by either: (a) closely packed buttonhole stitching (French needle laces – point de France, Argentan, Alençon); (b) spaced buttonhole stitching (Belgian needle laces – point de Venise and Point de gaze, see fig. 45); or (c) oversewing (Burano). They successfully covered over ends of thread left during the filling in of the design, and also concealed the points of junction of the bars. Flat Venetian laces had no additional cordonnet and, though the work continued to be superlatively skilful, they were often regarded as degenerate forms.

Lifting off the lace
Proceed as for Reticella (Chapter 3, page 39).

Variations

Venetian lace was the first of the true needle laces, and nearly all subsequent forms borrowed heavily from its inspiration. Its beautifully decorative yet unobtrusive bars blended harmoniously with the design, enhancing its richness.

France, towards the end of the seventeenth century, disciplined the free attachments of Venice into a ground of branching bars organized into large meshes, some 6mm ($\frac{4}{16}$ in) in diameter, and referred to as a 'meshwork of bars'. In the early eighteenth century, the enforced evenness of arrangement was combined with a reduction in the size of the enclosed spaces to 2 mm ($\frac{1}{16}$ in). The characteristic picots of point de France were discarded and what resulted was the fine buttonhole-stitched mesh ground of a lace known as Argentan (fig. 46).

Some indication of the enormous variety of forms which sprang from the three-dimensional

46a *Working from left to right, a series of buttonhole stitches are looped over a foundation cord. The sides of adjoining meshes are twisted. Pass the needle under the foundation cord as for detached buttonhole stitch (fig 00, page 00). Tilt the tip of the needle to the left, taking it under and over the thread. Pull the needle gently through the twists, and go on to the next stitch.*

46b *The Belgian Point de gaze mesh ground. Buttonhole stitches are made in every row. The sides of the meshes in rows 1, 3 etc., usually have two twists; those in rows 2, 4 etc. a single twist.*

46c *Alençon mesh ground of the type known as* **reseau ordinaire** *(mainly eighteenth century). In the rows running from right to left, no buttonhole stitches are worked; and the return thread running from right to left is not straight, but is twisted twice around each loop of the previous row.*

46d *Heavier mesh grounds are made over a detached buttonhole stitch supporting skeleton. Left to right: buttonhole stitches. Right to left: a straight return, but with the thread taken inside the loops instead of lying outside them (compare fig. 31 page 39).*

46e *Alençon* **brides tortillées** *mesh ground. The skeleton of (d) is overcast on every side of every mesh, giving it a much heavier appearance (nineteenth century). Beginning at the left, overcast side 1. Take the thread up side 2, loop it over the foundation cord, overcast down. Overcast side 3, take the thread down side 4, overcast up. Repeat to end of row. In the next row, beginning at the right, proceed in a similar way, though there is only one set of vertical sides to be worked. At each, carry the thread straight up, then overcast down.*

46f *Argentan* **brides bouclées***. This is similar to (e), except that every side of every mesh is covered with buttonhole stitches instead of being overcast. (Mainly eighteenth century).*

baroque laces of seventeenth-century Venice can be seen on page 71.

Bar grounds in general are associated with bold designs and heavy laces. In lighter work the solid design areas are smaller, with less intensive packing of stitches and little raised work. A mesh ground then shows the design to better advantage, as well as linking the reduced motifs more securely together. A variety of mesh forms are illustrated in figs. 46 a-f.

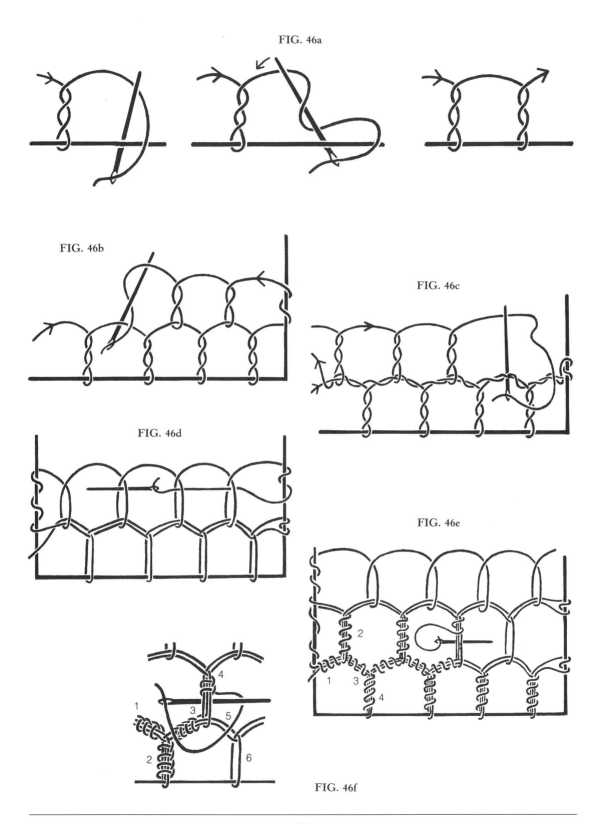

FIG. 46a

FIG. 46b

FIG. 46c

FIG. 46d

FIG. 46e

FIG. 46f

The lace pillow

A great advantage of needle-made laces from the lacemaker's point of view is that they are small enough to be carried around, while the stitches are sufficiently simple and repetitive to be worked in odd moments. However, for larger pieces, or for professional work, it is an advantage to have a fixed support in place of the hand support allowed for by a cloth or card. Fig. 47 illustrates the traditional support used in Burano.

FIG. 47

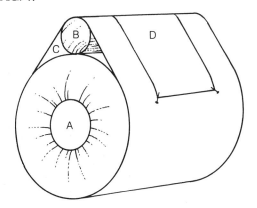

47 Burano cushion or pillow for needle lace-making. A cylindrical pillow (A) is topped by a wooden baton (B). The two are bound together by a cloth (C) wrapped around them. The pattern (D) rests over the baton and is secured by pins. By gradually moving the baton beneath the encircling cloth, the lacemaker can support different areas of the lace in turn.

Fake Venetian laces

In the later nineteenth century, not only were copies of seventeenth-century Venetian laces

FIG. 48

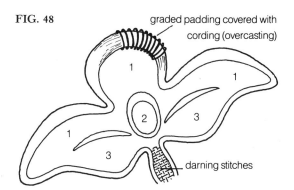

48 A design for fake Venetian lace, sometimes known as **punto a cordello***.*

made by traditional or near-traditional needle lace techniques, but other methods such as darning were also used to fill in the solid parts of the design. This saved a great deal of time and effort and, therefore, money, since making perfectly even and precisely-placed buttonhole stitches requires far more practice, concentration and patience than darning does. The bars linking the design areas together are corded or overcast, which is less labour intensive than covering them with buttonhole stitching.

The results were especially deceptive when antique designs were used in combination with heavily padded outlines and selected fillings worked in fancy buttonhole stitches as in fig. 48. Here area (1) and the stem are filled with darning stitches. Lay straight threads horizontally across the section linking them securely to the foundation cords on either side. Work the needle over and under these strands in a darning manner, twisting them around the relevant foundation cords above and below for anchorage (fig. 49).

Opposite A baby cap in coarsely-woven linen, with Reticella insets: the long straps, bordered with bobbin lace, support the baby's head (Scandinavian, eighteenth century). A triangle of antique design, worked over a scaffolding of plaited strands, nineteenth century. A large handkerchief, c.1700, recentred: the Punto in aria trimming features scrolls and lions; in the buttonhole-stitch inset, hounds and turkeys flank a central carnation.

FIG. 49

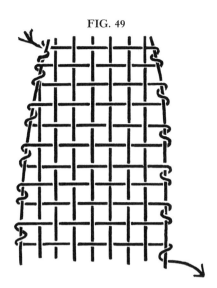

FIG. 50

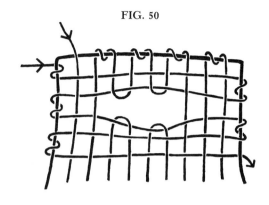

49 *Filling area (1) with darning stitches.*

50 *Making minute windows in the solid areas of the design.*

Tiny openings can be used to break up the solidity (fig. 50). This produces an impression of stitch 4, page 47. Stitches 2 and 3, also described on page 47, or any buttonhole stitches from Chapters 6 or 7, can be used for areas 2 and 3. Compare this technique with Halas lace, pages 64-70.

Once the general principles of making needle laces are understood, any lace and any stitch variation can be copied, simply by examining it closely, noting how the threads twist and the stitches are grouped, and trying out needle movements, over a piece of soft felt for example, until the right effect is obtained. In this way, laces superficially as different as Alençon, Point de gaze, Youghal and Burano, can all be analyzed, and with patience, practice and a little skill, recreated.

Point de France began in 1665 as a copy of Venetian gros point, aimed to block the costly importations which were causing a trade deficit. Venetian lacemakers were settled in areas such as Alençon, already celebrated for its skilled needlewomen. When the state monopoly of the early point de France expired in 1675, French designers replaced the bold flow of archaic stems and three-dimensional blooms linked by short bars, with a stylized symmetry of meticulous figures set in a disciplined meshwork. This form was worn at court for flounces, aprons, cravats and ruffles until 1700. Fine linen thread was used.

Ground: a meshwork of bars, as fig. 42, but less regular. Average mesh size, 6 to 8 mm, each side with one or two picots (fig. 71e).

Solid areas: detached buttonhole stitch with a straight return (fig. 31), close form. Pore-like openings (*portes*) may be present, as in all the derivatives (fig. 40).

Decorative stitches: typically Venetian, see figs. 38 to 40, 63 d-h.

Opposite Centre Venetian gros point, seventeenth century. The fine linen thread has a waxy sheen, and the bars are shaped into thin stems. **Top Left** Venetian rose point. The design is congested, linked by a structured ground of starry bars. **Below Left** Fake Venetian lace, darning stitch replaces buttonhole stitches in the solid areas. **Right** The lace is worked over a pattern inked on parchment.

Cordonnet: main design areas flat, with a double foundation cord but no additional cordonnet. The flower centres may have raised circles, plain or with picots.

Argentan, Normandy. One of the original point de France centres which developed a distinctive form soon after 1700. It was worn at the French court until about 1770, when the lighter Alençon lace replaced it.

Ground: meshes uniform, approximately 2 mm in diameter, with no picots (fig. 47f).

Solid areas: smaller than in point de France, but the same stitch.

Decorative stitches: Venetian, but lighter and more angular, the threads tensioned. Sometimes covering wide areas, with the solid parts embedded in them.

Cordonnet: a thread is attached over the foundation cord by close buttonhole stitching, giving the appearance of a raised rim.

Alençon, fifty miles south of Argentan, produced *vélin* (Antique Cutwork made on parchment) in the early seventeenth century. This was called 'Alençon lace'; so was the point de France later made there; so was a distinct form, shown in portraits e.g. of Marie Antoinette in the 1770s, and Napoleon I in 1804; and bought by the Empress Eugenie in 1855 and 1867. The date of origin of this distinctive type is uncertain: matching actual appearances with antique lace names necessarily involves some guesswork. Cotton thread was used from the 1850s when machine-spun counts of 400 to 500 were available, while fine linen thread was difficult to obtain.

Ground: (a) reseau ordinaire (fig. 46c); (b) brides tortillées (fig. 46d,e), regarded as a labour-saving imitation of the Argentan ground.

Solid areas: small units. Eighteenth century, detached buttonhole stitch with a straight return, close form. Mid-nineteenth century, the open form of this stitch alternates with closer areas where the stitches are smaller and the return threads tightened.

Decorative stitches: characteristic enclosures along the free border hold a diminutive form of reseau ordinaire, known as 'petit reseau'; or a trelliswork of buttonhole-stitched bars fringed with picots; or minute (1mm) circles, known as 'O', bristling with picots referred to as noses. They may be arranged in lines (*O à nez en queue*), in diamond frames (*O encadrés*), with eight radiating 'legs' (*O à huit pattes*), and so on.

Cordonnet: as in Argentan, but with many additional picots looped over horsehair, or human hair, to keep the size uniform.

Burano, five miles north of Venice. Little is known of its productions before 1873, when a school was established. Exquisite copies of seventeenth-century Venetian laces were made, and quantities of less exquisite commercial laces incorporating Alençon features. A pale écru cotton was used.

Ground: Alençon reseau ordinaire (fig. 46c), with the return threads pulled tightly, making the meshes square instead of hexagonal.

Solid areas: detached buttonhole stitch with a straight return, close form.

Decorative stitches: both French and Venetian appear. Entire flowers may be worked in fancy stitches. Picots are rare; horsehair is not used.

Cordonnet: a strand of thickish thread is couched over the foundation cord.

5
ENGLISH NEEDLE LACES

*T*HE NEEDLE LACES developed in France and Flanders in the seventeenth and eighteenth centuries, and in Burano, Hungary, Spain, Austria and Ireland in the nineteenth and twentieth centuries, all made use of the detached buttonhole stitch with a straight return for the solid areas of design, just as the Venetian laces had during their grand flourishing. Decorative variations were created by: varying the number of twists along the sides of the loops; varying the groupings of the stitches so that they formed patterns; working loops always from left to right, with the needle pointing away, but returning from right to left either with loops, by a straight thread, or by twisting the thread around the loops of the previous row (whipped return). In all, over sixty types of detached buttonhole stitch have been identified in Venetian laces and their derivatives.

In contrast, the design areas of English needle laces do not use the detached buttonhole stitch at all. Instead they are worked with a stitch of their own, known as hollie stitch, or hollie point (*point* being the French for stitch). Essentially this is a twisted buttonhole stitch, which, when tightened, gives the appearance of a knot.

◇DISTRIBUTION Laces made exclusively of hollie stitch are restricted to England. They take two forms, a very distinctive lace known as Hollie point, and the closely related 'English Needle Lace'. The use of this stitch form for both the solid and decorative areas of the design is an easy way of distinguishing English needle laces from any other.

◇HISTORY Hollie point appeared soon after 1700. It was used solely as a kind of seaming or insertion lace for the fine linen caps, shirts, bibs and mittens of christening sets ordered for the offspring of noble families.

Designs are pictoral and often biblical, with representations of Adam and Eve, and the good shepherd (in eighteenth-century dress); the crown of glory, dove of peace, olive branch, vine leaves and bunches of grapes are also common symbols. This characteristic provides a historical link with English stumpwork pictures of the first half of the seventeenth century, where the layered garments of men and women consisted of buttonhole-stitch fabrics worked in coloured silks, with representations of Solomon, Hagar and other Old Testament figures dressed in the latest fashion of the Stuart Court.

Dated Hollie point laces are eighteenth century, except for one or two examples from the early nineteenth century; these are of inferior quality, however, and the advent of the far prettier Ayrshire work (Chapter 2) in 1815 soon put an end to their flagging production. English Needle Lace appears to be restricted to the second half of the seventeenth century. Several pieces bear the date 1689.

◇MATERIALS   A fine, medium-length, blunt-tipped needle; fairly tightly spun thread which will cling rather than slip; foundation cords; coloured backing fabric; a drawn design, or numbered instructions.

Type 1: Hollie Point

In early eighteenth-century Hollie Point, the linen thread is very fine and the stitches are packed so tightly together than there might be more than 4,500 per square inch.

Hollie Point is unusual among needle laces not only in its stitch but also in the form of its design. Unlike Venetian-style laces (Chapter 4) it has no open ground, no solid design areas, and no decorative filling stitches. It is in fact just row after row of close hollie stitches and the design is formed by the holes or gaps left between stitches. Thus the final lace has the appearance of pinholes pricked in a solid fabric.

The Design

An extremely simple design has been chosen for practising the stitch and the formation of holes.

The work is much too dense to be done over a pattern. Instead, the sequence of stitches can be followed from a chart; or the instructions can be written out in the manner of a knitting pattern, for example, work 4, miss 1, work 2, miss 1, work 4, and so on, but this takes up a lot of space.

Fig. 51 shows a chart for a simple diamond shape. On the right only the stitch rows are numbered; the straight returns are omitted.

FIG. 51

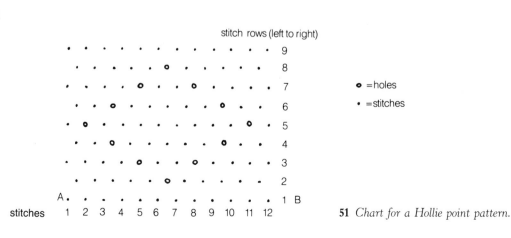

51 *Chart for a Hollie point pattern.*

58

Setting up the work

This is basically the same as the method described for Venetian lace (Chapter 4), but much simpler. Only the overall shape of the piece needs to be outlined with a foundation cord, not each part of the design.

Take a piece of coloured fabric which will show up the threads as you work. Cover it with architect's linen which the needle can slide over without penetrating so that you will not be hampered by the needle getting caught in the support. Mark out the total size of the lace on the linen, prick paired holes along this outline, then couch down foundation cords by passing the needle and thread through these holes (fig. 52).

In a variation, unique to Hollie point, the foundation cord was entirely omitted and the lace was worked directly into the baby garment that it was intended to decorate. This technique is described on pages 61-62.

The stitch

Hollie stitch is in fact very similar to the twisting of the sides of the meshes in Alençon *reseau ordinaire* (fig. 46a), but because the thread is held differently the final effect does not look the same. Instuctions for working the stitch are given in fig. 53a-g.

FIG. 52

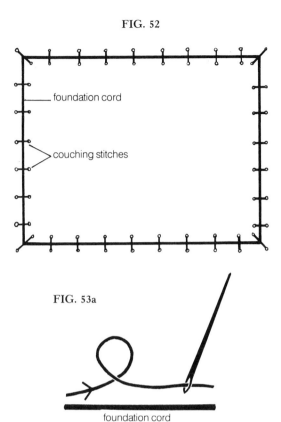

FIG. 53a

FIG. 53b

foundation cord

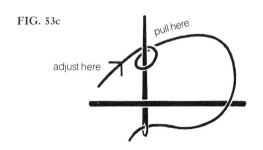

FIG. 53c

pull here

adjust here

52 *Foundation cord couched to a support such as green cloth, to outline the Hollie point area.*

53a–g *Hollie stitch. Fix the thread to the lower left-hand corner foundation cord at A with an overhand knot (see fig. 17, page 24). Work from left to right with the needle pointing away from you.*
53a *Make a loop. Note that the outgoing thread crosses over the incoming thread.*
53b *Slide the tip of the needle under the foundation cord, over the crossed threads, and under the loop.*
53c *Tighten the twist around the needle by pulling on the outgoing thread. At the same time adjust the interval between this stitch and the left-hand foundation cord, or the previous stitch, by edging the needle along to the left as necessary.* (cont. overleaf.)

FIG. 53d **FIG. 53e** **FIG. 53f**

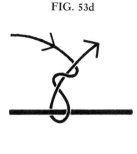

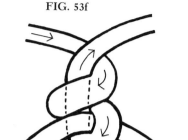

53d *Place your left thumb firmly over the twist as the thread is pulled through so that it does not slip out of place.*

53e *(enlarged). As you tighten the stitch further, the loop will slide down over the outgoing thread giving the appearance of a knot around it. This 'knot' should rest just above the foundation cord or, later, above the return thread of the previous row.*

53f *(enlarged). Tightening the stitch further will spread and distort it, obscuring the exit thread and giving a false impression of the path taken. This is the most usual appearance in the more solid areas of eighteenth-century Hollie point laces, where the stitches are closely packed and tension is high. Where gaps are left to form the design, the tension is reduced and the stitches ease out, appearing as shown in (d).*

53g *When the design requires larger holes, the tension is left slack and an additional twist is added.*

FIG. 53g

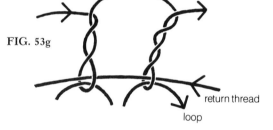

return thread

loop

Working the lace

Refer to fig. 51.

First stitch row Work twelve hollie stitches from A to B. Take the thread in a twist around the right-hand foundation cord, carry it back to the left-hand side just above the loops of the first row. Twist it around the left-hand foundation cord.

Second stitch row Work five stitches, taking the tip of the needle under both the appropriate loop of the previous row and the straight return thread. Miss one loop, leaving a longer length of thread between. This will pass over two stitches (fig. 54). Continue to the right-hand side working five stitches. Twist around the foundation cord. Make a straight return to the left-hand side.

Third stitch row Work four, miss one loop. Work two stitches into the loop previously missed. Miss one loop. Work four stitches.

Continue in this way, following the chart in fig. 51. Miss stitches as indicated, and fill them in again in the next stitch row. Remember to twist the thread around the foundation cord at the beginning and end of every row, and that every alternate row is a straight return.

On the ninth stitch row, take the loops over the top of the foundation cord. The piece is now complete.

Longer strips can be made by marking out a

FIG. 54a

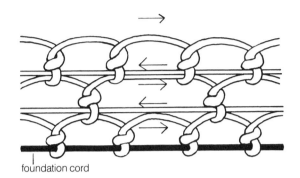

foundation cord

FIG. 54b

foundation cord

54a *Hollie stitch showing one loop missed in the second row of loops, then filled in with two new stitches in the third row of loops.*
54b *In the actual lace the stitches are extremely close together.*

larger area with the foundation cord and then either repeating the same design, or working a series of different ones. A rectangular shape is not essential: the lace for the crowns of the bonnets was usually circular.

In eighteenth-century Hollie point it was most usual for the rows of stitches to be worked across the short axis of the strip so that they would lie horizontally in the finished lace. However they were sometimes worked lengthwise.

Lifting off the lace

Working from the reverse side, cut through the tacking and couching threads which hold the lace to its support.

Mounting the lace

The completed band of Hollie point was traditionally attached by tiny overcasting stitches down the centre line of a baby cap or at the shoulders of a christening shirt, so that it acted as a seaming lace, joining two pieces of linen together. The cap sides, or the shirt shoulders, would already be prepared with a narrow (2 mm

[$\frac{1}{16}$ in]) hem-stitched border such as is shown in fig. 55a.

Working the lace within the garment

A row of larger than usual hollie stitches is worked directly on to the hemmed edges of the linen garment, entirely around the area to be filled with lace (figs. 55a and b, and 56). Work the Hollie point as before, but taking the threads through the loops instead of around the foundation cord at the end of each row.

Type 2: English Needle Lace

Although in the generic sense English needle laces include Hollie point, the term is normally used in a restricted sense for lace which differs from Hollie point in several ways, as follows:
◇The lace may be worked over an inked or printed pattern. In fact, little more than its distinctive stitch and a certain lack of artistry in much of the work, distinguishes it from a flat Venetian lace.

FIG. 55a

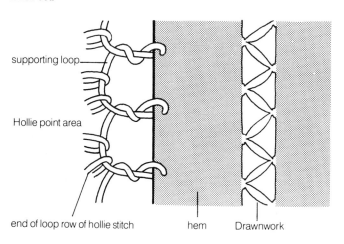

supporting loop

Hollie point area

end of loop row of hollie stitch   hem   Drawnwork

55 and 56 From an eighteenth-century baby cap.

55a Hollie point made without a foundation cord, but with each pair of rows linked around hollie stitch loops worked into the cap hem using a pointed needle.
55b The left-hand support loops showing the hitching over of hollie stitch rows (L) and straight return rows (R).
L = left to right. R = right to left.

56 The top of the Hollie point, using the technique shown in fig. 55. The panel is finished by a row of much larger stitches hooked through pre-made loops along the fabric of the cap.

FIG. 55b

R
L
R
L
R
L
R

FIG. 56

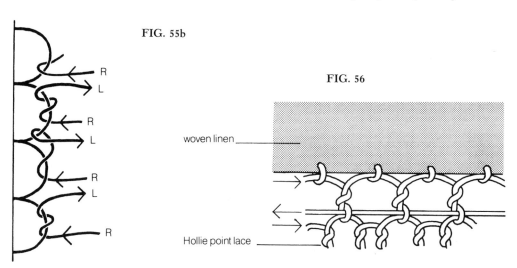

woven linen

Hollie point lace

◇Each part of the design has to be outlined with a foundation cord.
◇It has solid design areas.
◇The design areas are enriched with decorative 'twisted' filling stitches of six or more different kinds, though they are considerably less varied than the corresponding stitches in Venetian laces.
◇The lace has a structured openwork ground of bars.

Each individual motif of the design is worked as for Hollie point, the closely-packed hollie stitches being arranged in rigidly parallel rows, and linked over foundation cords at either end. Such solid areas alternate with lighter ones where the stitches have been grouped in various ways to create patterns of holes.

Three examples of such decorative stitches are shown in fig. 57.

Supporting threads for the bars are looped over the foundation cords of neighbouring motifs, buttonhole-stitched over, and decorated with little crowns and picots which are very similar to those described for Venetian laces (Chapter 4, page 49).

57 *Three decorative stitches found in seventeenth-century English Needle Laces. For clarity the stitches have been spaced more widely apart.*

FIG. 57a

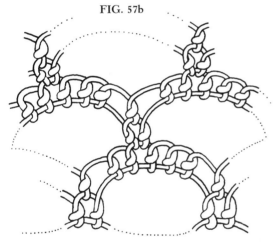

rows of twisted buttonhole stitch

straight return thread

FIG. 57b

FIG 57c

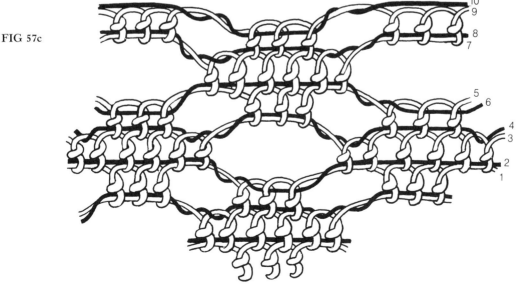

57a *Part of a small diamond pattern with the stitches grouped in pairs (work two, miss two). Alternatively the stitches can be grouped and missed in threes.*

57b *A two-row pattern making larger holes. Row 1: work right across. Row 3: miss two, work two, miss six, work two, miss six, etc. Row 5: work right across working five stitches into each long loop and one into the short loop of each pair of stitches of row 3. Row 7: repeat row 3. Because of the tension of the stitches the holes are pulled out into oval shapes making the work appear much more complex than it really is. Rows 2, 4, 6, etc., are straight returns which have been omitted in the drawing for clarity.*

57c *A ten-row diamond pattern. Begin at the bottom left-hand side, fastening the thread to the foundation cord. Row 1: miss two (two-loop gap), work three, miss two, work three, continue to end. Row 2: make a straight return but secure the threads over the loops in the gap areas. Row 3: work six stitches so that the central two take in the loops and return thread of rows 1 and 2, as shown in 7(c), miss three stitches making a long loop, continue to end. Row 4: carry the return thread back to the left-hand side securing it around or within the loops as indicated so that it cannot splay out and spoil the shape of the holes. Row 5: miss two, work three, to end (as row 1). Row 6: as row 2. Row 7: repeat row 3, but begin by missing three loops, then work six stitches so that the diamond-shaped block will alternate with the previous one. Row 8: repeat row 4. Row 9: repeat row 1. Row 10: repeat row 2.*

6
HALAS

CHAPTERS 4 and 5 were concerned with 'pure' needle laces in which both the design and ground areas consisted entirely of buttonhole stitches. Halas, though made with a sewing needle, has a mixture of techniques. Its solid design motifs are worked in darning stitch so that they give the impression of woven cloth, or the clothstitch found in bobbin laces. The varied buttonhole stitches are restricted to the openwork ground or to decorative fillings where they form delightful highlights contrasting with the plain 'weave'.

◇DISTRIBUTION & HISTORY

Halas lace originated in Hungary (where it is known as Haläser) and is most strongly associated with the town of Kiskunhalas from which it takes its name.

Hungary has a long tradition of embroidered lace, most especially Drawnwork, and also of bobbin lace. References from the early seventeenth century speak of a law being passed forbidding women to make bobbin laces as these were distracting them from their more urgent and practical duties, such as ploughing the fields or spinning.

Needle-made lace, however, played no part in this ancient cottage tradition. Halas lace was an entirely twentieth-century innovation, created by one man, Arpád Dekáni, who was inspired by the Art Nouveau movement of the turn of the century which, in all European countries, injected a new vitality into lace design. Much of Dekáni's work was pictorial: cockerels, peacocks, doves, swans, floating water-lillies and dancing figures.

The technical features of Halas derive from three distinct sources:

(a) The plain-weave linen forming the designs of Hungarian Drawnwork.

(b) Punto a cordello, the labour-saving Venetian gros point made in Burano at the end of the nineteenth century, which substituted a darning stitch for the slow and tedious infilling of closely-worked detached buttonhole stitches (page 52).

(c) The multitude of decorative stitches used in antique Venetian gros points to give lightness and buoyancy to what might otherwise have been an overpoweringly heavy lace.

◇MATERIALS & STITCHES

Dekáni's early work, 1902-6, used coloured silks to work the twelve types of buttonhole stitch which together formed both the decorative fillings and the ground. The foundation cords were thick, emphasising the outline of the design, though the lace as a whole was flat with no additional raised work. The free, i.e. the unattached border of the lace, was often decorated with picots. Within a few years, however, white linen thread took the place of colour and silk; thinner foundation cords were used; the picots of the border were omitted; and the number of decorative stitches increased, little by little, to a total of sixty.

Any of the decorative stitches of Venetian lace can be used. As with all the buttonhole stitches, once the general principle of making them is understood, they are easily copied from actual laces, for example museum specimens. The 'clothwork' or solids design areas are made of darning stitch, and look exactly like a woven cloth. Linen thread of fine count is used in true Halas lace, but this makes the work very laborious for a complete beginner and, as with all laces, there is no harm in trying out the technique in thick thread, either white or coloured, whichever is found to be easier.

You will also need a blunt-tipped needle, foundation cord, pricker, traced design and a support.

FIG. 58

58 *The pattern. The stitches to be used in the areas numbered 2–11 are shown in fig. 63. The areas marked 1 are empty circles.*

Setting up the lace

Trace or photocopy the pattern (fig. 58) onto paper. Back with a firm layer of cloth, and cover with translucent architect's linen.

Prick small holes on either side of every line of the pattern. Couch a foundation cord around this outline (see fig. 30, page 38), taking the stitches through the linen, the pattern and the cloth below (fig. 59). The areas marked (1) on the pattern are empty circles. Arrange the cord around these circles and the rest of the pattern so that it keeps its continuity and the number of joins is minimized (fig. 60).

Pin the supporting cloth firmly along its top edge to a lacemaker's pillow. A sloping polystyrene or softboard block will do almost as well. Traditionally a wooden frame filled with sand and covered with canvas was used, its heaviness keeping it rock-steady as the work progressed. The idea is simply to allow the handling of the cloth and lace to be restricted to small areas, and to bring it to a convenient height.

Note If the design looks too formidable, a part of it can be selected, and the smaller piece of supporting cloth can be held in the hand.

The 'woven' areas

These are the unnumbered parts in fig. 58, that is, the eagle and the bordering scrolls.

To create the 'warps' Beginning at the left-hand upper foundation cord of the area, take the thread straight down to, and around, the lower foundation cord. Take the thread back up again, twist around the cord, and return to the bottom cord. Continue in this way until the whole area is filled with evenly spaced vertical threads (fig. 61).

FIG. 59

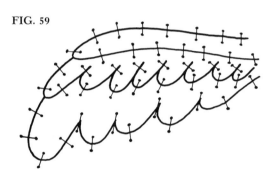

59 *The eagle's wing showing foundation cord held down by couching threads.*

FIG. 60

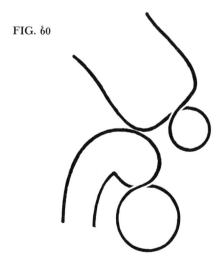

60 *Taking the foundation cord around area 1.*

FIG. 61a

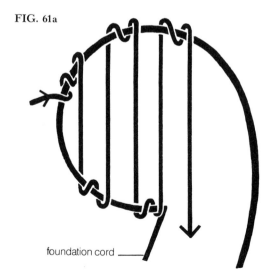

foundation cord

61a *Laying the 'warps'.*

FIG. 61b

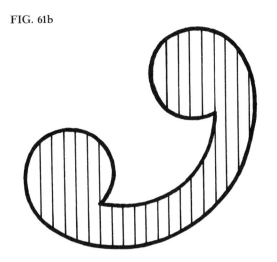

61b *The warps completed.*

FIG. 62b

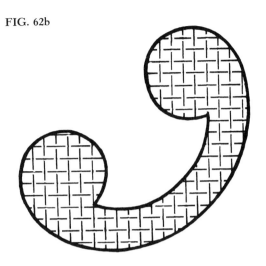

62b *A 'woven' area completed.*

To make the 'wefts' Now work in a similar manner in the horizontal direction, weaving over and under the vertical threads, and twisting around the foundation cords at the right- and left-hand sides. These vertical and horizontal darning threads must be precisely at right angles to each other (fig. 62).

FIG. 62a

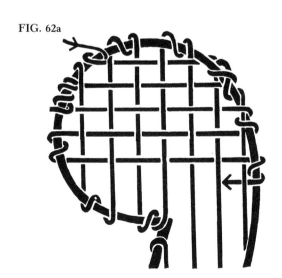

62a *Darning in the 'wefts'.*

The buttonhole stitches

To make the openwork part of the lace, areas 2 to 10 of fig. 58 are filled with decorative buttonhole stitches. The stitches shown in fig. 63 a-c, which have already been described in Chapters 3 and 4, could, for simplicity, be used for all the areas; but, for more ambitious workers, further buttonhole stitches are described (fig. 63 d-i) including a special stitch for area 11 (fig. 63j). All are traditional to Halas lace, and all except 63j to the earlier Venetian laces.

In each case, work the first row of stitches over a foundation cord, with the needle pointing away from you, beginning in the left-right direction. If needle-towards is preferred, turn the page upside down. Left and right directions are also reversible in most instances (see Introduction, page 7).

Lifting off the lace

Remove the pins which hold the cloth to the pillow. Cut through the couching stitches from the reverse side. This releases the foundation cords and the lace can now be lifted off. The pattern itself can be used again. Fasten off loose thread ends at the back of the work.

63a–j *Stitches to fill areas 2–10 in fig. 58.*

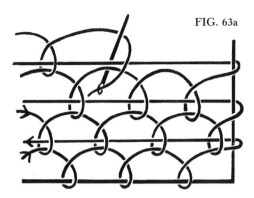

FIG. 63a

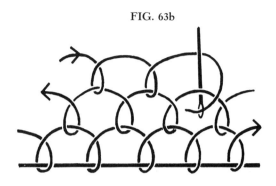

FIG. 63b

63a *Detached buttonhole stitch with a straight return, open form.*

63b *Detached buttonhole stitch, or single Brussels stitch.*

FIG. 63c

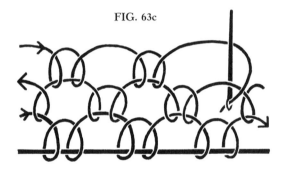

FIG. 63d

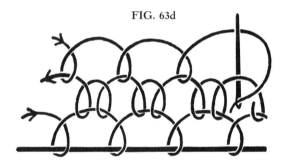

63c *Double Brussels stitch called, in Halas, double Cumanian stitch.*

63d *Known in Halas as Garland stitch. This is similar to (c) except that rows of double buttonhole stitch alternate with single. The loops of the single stitches are naturally longer than those of the double.*

FIG. 63e

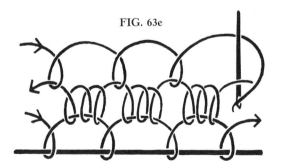

63e *Known in Halas as triple buttonhole stitch. This is similar to (d) except that groups of three stitches alternate with single stitches in successive rows.*

FIG. 63f

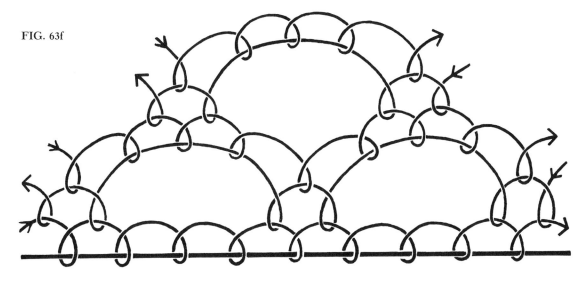

63f *Known as Pea stitch or Roman net. The general idea is similar to (d) and (e), but where stitches are missed the loops are pulled upwards to form larger holes. If the work is supported on a pillow, pins can be used to hold these longer loops in place, so ensuring that they are all of equal size. Row 1: work detached buttonhole stitches right across the foundation cord, from left to right.*

Row 2: starting at the right-hand side, work two stitches, miss two loops leaving a long curved thread between, work two stitches, miss two loops, continue to the end. Row 3: make a full row of stitches, working three into each long loop, and one into the single loop between. Repeat rows 1 to 3 throughout making successive holes alternate, as shown.

FIG. 63g

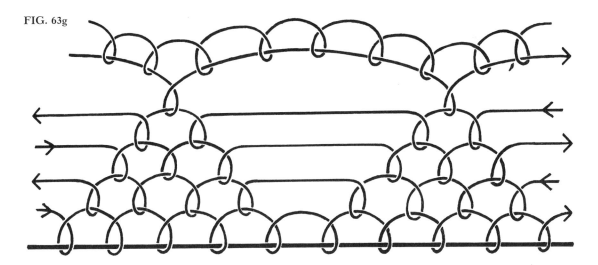

63g *Pyramid stitch or Vandyke stitch. Row 1: work detached buttonhole stitch right across the foundation cord, from left to right. Twist the thread around the foundation cord. Row 2: miss one loop, make stitches in the next four loops, miss one, work four, etc. Row 3 (left to right): work three stitches into the loops of each group of four stitches of row 2. Row 4: work two stitches into*

the loops of each group of three stitches of row 2. Lengthen the unused thread between the groups in each row so that the triangular shapes are not distorted. Row 5: work one stitch into the loop of each group of two stitches of row 4. Row 6: work right across, making five stitches along each loop between the single stitches of row 5. Rows 7–12: repeat rows 1–6 so that the pyramids alternate.

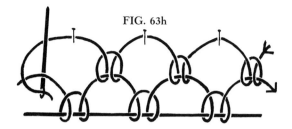

FIG. 63h

63h *Work a pair of detached buttonhole stitches over the foundation cord. Pass the needle and thread over and under a spacer, such as a thin knitting needle. Work a pair of stitches. Pass the thread around the spacer. Continue to the end. Work back again from right to left in the same manner, so that the pairs of stitches alternate with those of the previous row. Repeat these two rows.*

FIG. 63i

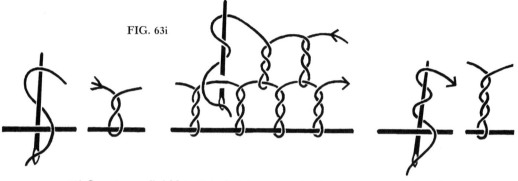

63i *Sometimes called Net stitch. Stitches are worked in every row, as indicated. There can be one, two or three twists.*

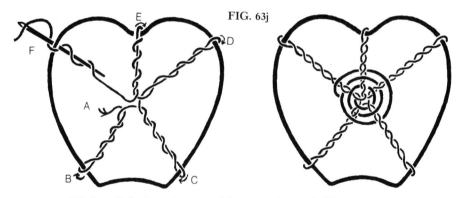

FIG. 63j

63j *Area 11. Begin at the centre, A, leaving a short end of thread which can later be stitched into the back of the wheel. Take the thread over the foundation cord at B, and twist around on the return journey to the centre. Repeat for C, D, E and F. Now weave the needle in and out of these five strands in a circular direction until a small core like the hub of a wheel is completed. Fasten off the thread on the reverse side.*

Opposite Venetian lace derivatives. **Centre** A fan of Point de gaze with carved mother of pearl sticks. **Above left** A flounce of Youghal lace. **Above right** a handkerchief of French needle lace. **Below left to right** Alençon needle lace; a mat of point de Colbert with fleur de lys and satyr heads; a Burano bertha with large flowers of many decorative stitches; two medallions of Belgian point to Venise. All c.1860 to 1900.

7
TAPE-BASED LACES

*H*ALAS LACE diverged from true needle laces by having its solid areas of design filled with darning stitches instead of the typical detached buttonhole stitch with a straight return. Tape-based laces digress still further. Foundation cords are dispensed with, and their place is taken by tapes or braids of varying thickness, which are coiled, gathered or folded to follow a pattern. The pattern is printed or transferred onto a stiffened supporting fabric, which is, traditionally, a dense pink, green or blue calico over brown paper; or, alternatively, kid, synthetic leather, or tracing paper over oil cloth.

The tapes may be completely straight, or swollen at intervals like a string of sausages. They may be of a plain right-angled weave, or a twill weave with the threads passing diagonally, when they are known as braids. Both forms are usually made on a braiding machine; rarely, they are made with bobbins. They are nearly always edged along both borders with small perforations. These act as loops through which the needle can be passed to hang the buttonhole stitches which fill or link the various parts of the lace.

◇NAMES Tape-based laces have a seventeenth-century origin, when they were known as '*mezzo punto*' (literally 'half stitches' referring perhaps to their being only half made of stitches, half of tape). In their mid-nineteenth-century revival they were known as 'point laces' (*cf* Daisy Waterhouse Hawkins' *Old Point Lace and How to Copy It*, published in 1878, and sundry instructions in *The Illustrated Exhibitor* of 1852). 'Point' (French, meaning stitch) was at that time applied generally to all laces and so was inadequately specific for the new form. The terms 'Renaissance' and 'Mediaeval' used from the 1860s to the 1880s were 'Modern Point Lace worked with a very open Braid and only one type of stitch as a Filling'.

Further ambiguities were introduced by the use of place-names for variations either in the kind of tape used, in the design or in the

Opposite Above English Needle Lace, the design motifs linked by a ground of picoted bars, c.1689. **Below** A baby cap showing Hollie point used as a seaming lace, and dated 1739. The shepherd, in fitted coat, breeches and tricorn hat may represent the Good Shepherd. Compare the initials A.P. with the hollie point dating.

stitch-forms. Examples are : Battenburg, Branscombe, Honiton, Brussels Princess, Luxeuil, Belgian point de Milan, Limoges and Ardenza. Distinguishing features of some of these laces are given on page 85.

The general terms 'tape-based laces' or 'laces of pre-made tapes', though rather arid-sounding, are at least unlikely to be misunderstood.

◇HISTORY &
DISTRIBUTION

The use of pre-made tapes was a labour-saving device, as was the replacement of close buttonhole-stitching by darning in punto a cordello (page 52). The seventeenth-century mezzo punto is associated with Italy. The nineteenth-century copies were almost exclusively non-professional and non-commercial, a domestic time-passer with some practical application. Instructions for making them appeared worldwide in ladies' journals, and were carried to the Far East by missionaries. Thus the geographical source of any particular piece is impossible to determine with certainty unless its history is known.

The ambiguities of the names attached to tape-based laces, discussed above, also make it difficult to trace the history of the lace. It is said that in the 1850s, soon after the Irish potato famines, point lace was taught to women and children at Ardee, Co. Louth, under the name 'lacet' (French, meaning a narrow tape or braid). There was also a Mrs Mitchell of Soho Bazaar and Portman Square who described herself ambiguously as a 'Honiton Point Lace Manufacturer'; and a Mr William Barnard of Edgware Road from whom point lace collars could be had in white or écru, and which were 'by no means expensive'.

◇MATERIALS

Tapes or braids between 2 mm ($\frac{1}{16}$ in) and 1 cm ($\frac{6}{16}$ in) wide, bought by the metre. In the second half of the nineteenth century some fifty varieties were available, but the selection now is very restricted.

Smooth thread with a firm twist, its thickness to be consistent with that of the tape.

A pattern printed on cotton, or traced onto architect's linen, and tacked to a supporting cloth using a pointed needle. If no pattern is available the lace itself can be copied by covering it with brown paper and rubbing with charcoal. This will give an outline sufficiently clear to follow, and the stitches themselves can be worked directly from the lace.

A blunt-tipped needle for making the filling stitches, picots and bars.

◇STITCHES

Any of sixty or so buttonhole stitches. In addition, raised rings, English wheels, wheatsheaf stitch, *point de reprise* and many others are found in nineteenth-century tape-based laces.

Overcast or buttonhole-stitched bars.

A variety of picots.

64 *Pattern of a butterfly.*   **FIG. 64a**

64a *Body and upper wings. Beginning at (1) tack the tape onto the pattern, proceeding in the direction of the arrows until (2) is reached. Carry the tape across to (3). Continue to tack the tape onto the pattern, following the arrows until (4) is reached. Carry the tape across to (5). Tack in the direction of the arrows to (6). Cut the tape. For the body: begin at A, tack the tape in a double figure eight as shown, finishing at A. This will conceal some of the wing tape (see dotted lines). Stitch the two tape ends neatly together and hide beneath the crossing tape.*

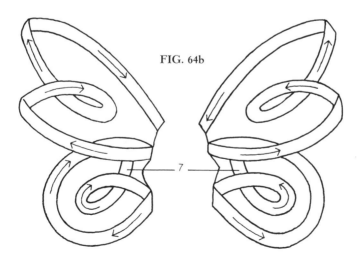

FIG. 64b

64b *Lower wings. Begin at (7) and follow the arrows through to the end.*

The outline of the design

The butterfly design shown in fig. 64 can be enlarged for use as a scarf or jabot ending, as a pincushion cover, or as an insertion into a dress or blouse. If it is to perch three-dimensionally on a cushion, or lampshade, or be converted by a pin at the back into a brooch, fine wire should be threaded through its entire outline and extended forwards from the head to make the knobbed antennae.

The design is worked in two parts: (a) the body and upper wings; (b) the lower wings which will, finally, be attached to the body, below the upper wings. Since the tape is straight and the outline of the design is not, the tape must be folded at angles and gathered at curves to fit the various convolutions.

Laying down the tape

Traditionally the lace is worked from the face side. Lay the tape along the outline of the pattern and attach it to the underlying cloth(s) with tacking stitches (fig. 65a). These are best kept to the middle of the tape, but where there is a sharp curve take them more to the outside. Where there is an angle fold the tape and hold it temporarily in position with a tacking stitch. After the tacking is completed, hem along the folds so that the stitches are almost invisible from the right side of the work. Run an overcasting stitch along the inner curve and pull the thread gently until the tape is reduced to the right length (fig. 65b).

As far as possible the tape should be made to go continuously round the outline, without joins. The arrows and numbers on fig. 64, and the directions given in the caption, show how close you can get to this ideal.

Filling in the design

The stitch possibilities are almost endless and the choice is free. Any of the decorative buttonhole stitches described in chapters 4, 5 or 6 could be used here, but for variety we have suggested

FIG. 65a

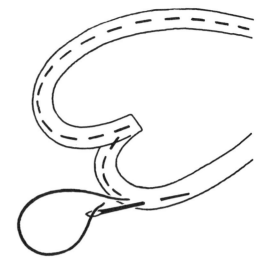

65a *The tape is held down with tacking stitches, which pass centrally where the tape is straight, and towards the outside at curves.*

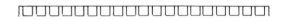

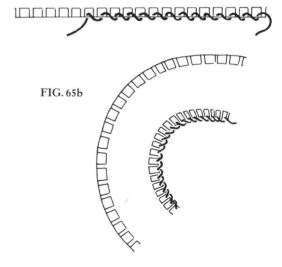

FIG. 65b

65b *(Detail.)* **Above** *Running in overcast stitches.* **Below** *Pulling the thread to make the tape fit the curve.*

FIG. 66

Venetian
edging

machine picot
border

66 *Key to the filling stitches (areas 1–8) and the position of the bars.*

seven further stitches, all fairly simple ones (fig. 66). The names used are traditional.

Area 1 English wheel/backstitch wheel (fig. 67a).

Area 2 Sorrento veining (fig. 67b).

Area 3 Point désir (fig. 67c)

Area 4 Point de Venise network (fig. 67d).

Area 5 English bars/insertion with bead stitches (fig. 67e)

Area 6 Point d'Alençon/plain Russian stitch (fig. 67f)

Area 7 Point de Sorrento (fig. 67g).

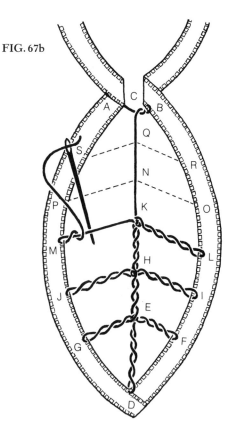

FIG. 67b

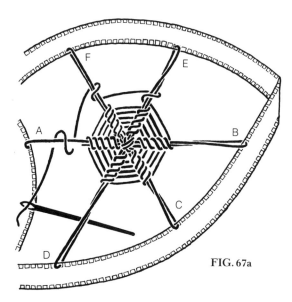

FIG. 67a

67a Area 1 *English wheel/backstitch wheel. Lay the six radii. Pass the thread from A to B, take the needle through a hole in the tape border and back to the centre. Knot the thread tightly to prevent slipping before taking it out to C, through a loop and back to the centre. Twist the thread over the knot, take it out to D, and proceed in this manner to E, then F, ending at the centre. Work in a circular manner, in and out of the radii, seven or eight times, passing the needle under each radius then back over it again as shown above.*

67b Area 2 *Sorrento veining. Attach the thread through a loop at A. Take it across to B, back to the mid-point C, and down to D. Return to point E, overcasting the central thread, and fix this position with a tight buttonhole stitch. Take the thread to F, overcast back to E, take the thread out to G, overcast to E, overcast to H, and so*

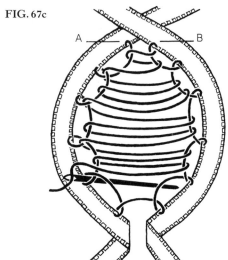

FIG. 67c

continue HI, overcast IH; HJ, overcast JH, overcast HK; and so on until the area is filled.

67c Area 3 *Point désir. Work around the inner border of the tape with detached buttonhole stitch, beginning at A and ending at B. Link the two rows of loops by overcasting, following the course shown above.*

FIG. 67d

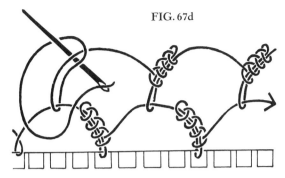

67d Area 4 *Point de Venise network. This is basically detached buttonhole stitch with four tight buttonhole stitches worked into the side of each loop where the threads cross. These four stitches may either begin at the upper end and work downwards towards the tape, or begin at the lower end next to the tape and work upwards. Work back again from right to left. Repeat these two rows until the space is filled.*

FIG. 67e

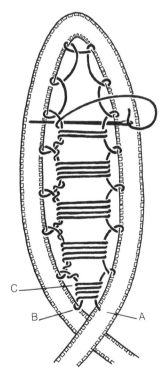

67e Area 5 *English bars/insertion with bead stitches. Work around the inner border of the tape with detached buttonhole stitches, beginning at A and ending at B. Every stitch must be exactly the same size, and the stitches of the two sides must be precisely opposite each other.*

67e cont.

Overcast the loop from B to its mid-point, then link opposing loops together with four overcast stitches, ending at C. Overcast the remainder of the first loop and the beginning of the next to the mid-point, and repeat until all the space is filled.

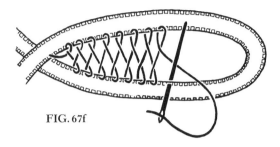

FIG. 67f

67f Area 6 *Point d'Alençon/plain Russian stitch. Fasten the thread at the lower left-hand corner. Carry the needle to the opposite side some three holes to the right and pass it through a hole in the tape with the needle pointing towards you. Pull the thread through, towards the right. Three holes along, pass the needle through the lower tape and proceed as shown above.*

FIG. 67g

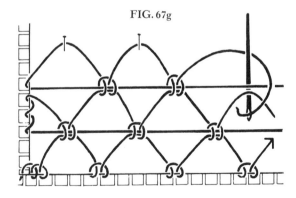

67g Area 7 *Point de Sorrento. Row 1: Fasten the thread to the lower left-hand corner of the area to be filled. Make two detached buttonhole stitches close together, then bend the thread in an acute loop, holding it in position with a pin. Continue to the end of the row, making all the stitches and loops of equal size. Row 2: carry the return thread straight back to the left-hand side and fasten it through a hole in the tape. Row 3: repeat row 1, working the pairs of stitches at the apex of each loop as shown above.*

The linking stitches

In most tape-based laces these take the form of bars. In the pattern they occupy the areas marked 8. Work as shown in fig. 68a. In two small sections to the inner sides of the upper wings the bars branch. Work these as shown in fig.68b.

Two other bar variations are shown in figs. 70a and b.

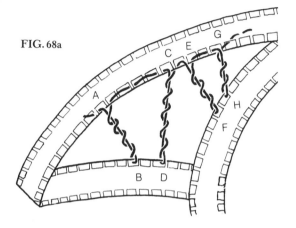

FIG. 68a

68a *Whipped or overcast bars. Fix the thread at A, take it across to B, overcast to A, making running stitches through the holes in the tape border to C. Take the thread across to D, overcast to C, and so on.*

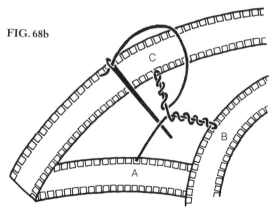

FIG. 68b

68b *Branching bars. Take a thread from A to B, leaving it slightly slack. Overcast it from B to the centre, then carry the thread up to C to tighten AB. Overcast C to the centre, then on to A.*

It is sometimes recommended that the bars be worked before the filling stitches, but incomplete nineteenth-century pieces show the bars left till last.

Decorations of bars and borders

Quite a variety of purls and picots are found in nineteenth-century tape-based laces. Their addition to the butterfly design is optional, and only one is decribed in detail here: Venetian edging (see fig. 69). A simple alternative to Venetian edging is to use machine picots which can be bought by the metre and stitched to the outer borders of the wings.

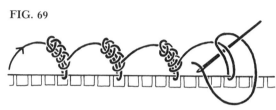

FIG. 69

69 *Venetian edging: this is similar to point de Venise network. (fig. 67d). Work as directed there, taking the point of the needle through evenly spaced holes along the tape, and making a single row only.*

Lifting off the lace

Cut through all the tacking stitches from the reverse side and lift the butterfly off the pattern. Stitch the lower pair of wings to the sides of the thorax, below the upper wings. In the interests of biological accuracy the wings should not be attached to the abdomen.

Variations

◇Bars may be buttonhole stitched instead of overcast. Two variations are shown in fig. 70.
◇Picots may consist of short chain-stitch projections, be overcast (straight or curved), buttonhole-stitched (straight, curved or Venetian), or knotted. These variations are described and illustrated in figs. 71 a-g.

70 *Bar variations.*

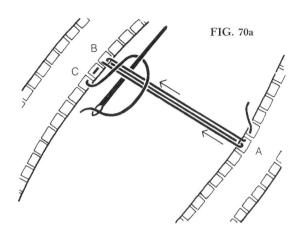

FIG. 70a

70a *Buttonholing over three strands, enlarged to show detail. Bring the thread out at A, take it across to B, back to A, across to B, then out at C and work buttonhole stitches to A.*

FIG. 70b

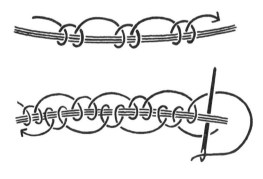

70b *Double buttonhole stitch over a supporting strand.* **Above** *Lay supporting strands, then work buttonhole stitches in pairs along the bar from left to right.* **Below** *Turn the lace upside down and work back, from left to right, fitting the pairs of stitches into the gaps left in row 1. This produces the appearance of small loops along either side of the bar.*
Double-buttonhole stitched bars are relatively rare in tape-based laces, but are a distinguishing feature of Flemish needle laces.

71a-g *Picot variations.*

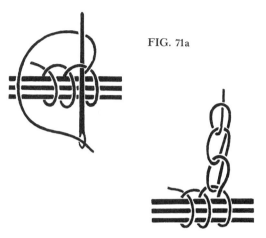

FIG. 71a

71a *Chain-stitch picot. Make buttonhole stitches to the middle of the bar. Take the needle through the loop of the previous stitch and make three or four chain-stitches. Take the thread back down the reverse side of the picot and continue to buttonhole stitch along the bar.*

FIG. 71b

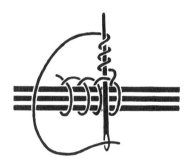

71b *Dots/pips/knobs. Make buttonhole stitches to the middle of the bar. Take the needle through the previous loop, wind the thread three or four times around the point, hold the thread down tightly with the thumb and pull the needle through the twists. Continue to buttonhole stitch along the bar.* (cont. overleaf.)

FIG. 71c

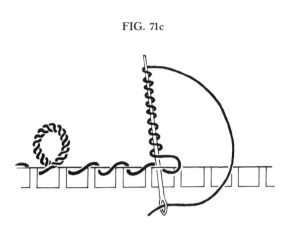

FIG. 71e

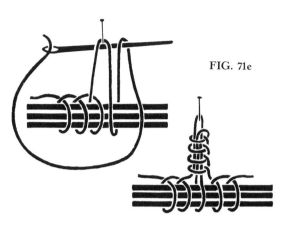

71c *Bullion stitch picots/Spanish edging. This can be added to a bar, or along the perforated border of the tape. Sew over the tape for three stitches. Insert the point of the needle back through the same hole, and wind the thread around it ten to twenty times, depending on the thickness of the thread. Draw the needle through the twists, pulling the thread tightly to form a small circle. Sew over the tape for three stitches, and repeat.*

71e *Venetian picots. Proceed as for (d) passing the needle under the three threads, but making the buttonhole stitch immediately next to the pin. Make a further two or three stitches down the thread, working back towards the bar.*

FIG. 71f

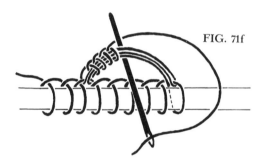

FIG. 71d

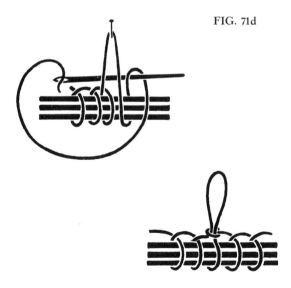

71f *Buttonhole ring/ring picot. Work buttonhole stitches to a little past half-way along the bar. Take the thread loosely back about five stitches and fasten it there. Bring the thread back, and return again to form a three-thread loop. Buttonhole stitch over this, then continue along the bar. These picots appear similar to (c), but are heavier and more commonly used for borders than bars.*

FIG. 71g

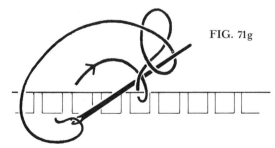

71d *Pinned picot. Make buttonhole stitches to the middle of the bar. Carry the thread up into a long loop and fix it in place with a pin. Insert the needle from left to right, under the three threads and over the fourth. Pull tightly, then continue buttonhole stitching along the bar.*

71g *Knotted picots. These are used for the outer edge of the lace. Follow the needle and thread movements shown above carefully.*

72 *Creating a mesh ground.*

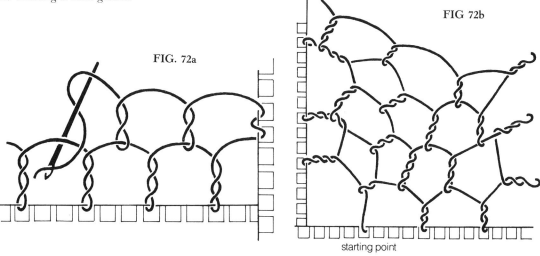

FIG. 72a

FIG 72b

starting point

72a *Tulle stitch. The sides of the loops may have one or two twists. Buttonhole stitches may be worked in every row, or may alternate with a whipped return (see fig. 46c, page 51). Guide-lines can be marked on the pattern to keep the rows straight.*
72b *Raleigh bars worked over a small area.*

◇The bar ground can be replaced by a mesh ground, which serves equally well to link the design areas together and gives a lighter more decorative appearance. This is characteristic of the Belgian tape-based lace known as point de Milan (fig. 72a). Raleigh bars form a more irregular network (fig. 72b).

◇The tapes may be shaped (fig. 73). Sausage-like forms of the nineteenth century were known as Honiton tapes. Brussels tapes of the twentieth century simulate flower petals and leaves, and may even give a convincing impression of a not very good bobbin lace.

◇The tapes may be stitched to a machine net instead of being linked by a bar- or mesh-ground. This form of appliqué work is especially characteristic of the lace known commercially as 'Brussels Princess'. The shaped tapes are basted to the pattern and support, but with the reverse side uppermost. The net is then stretched over them and held in place by random stitches. Finally net and tapes are linked together by running stitches which pass inconspicuously to the front of the lace and are knotted at the back so that they cannot slip and pucker (fig. 74). Tendrils of stem stitch and spots of satin stitch, or raised rings made of circles of thread buttonhole-stitched over, may be added if desired.

◇The choice of filling stitches can be varied. Mrs. Treadwin in 1874 listed some possibilities: plain clothing, mignonette, filet, pillar, loop, fleurette, trellice, box, double box, column, filigree, ladder, diamond, treble loop, square, chessboard, twist, and pointed treble. Unfortunately, the meaning of all these terms is lost in obscurity.

Note The use of more complex and very closely worked stitches does not necessarily render the lace prettier or more visually effective. Indeed – a great consolation for beginners – some of the most striking laces, such as the so-called Renaissance and Mediaeval, use coarse tapes and the minimum of hand-stitching worked in thick thread.

73 *Shaped tapes.*

FIG. 74a

FIG. 73a

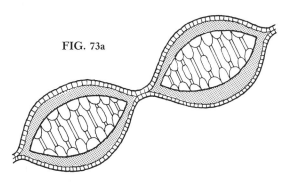

73a *Giant Honiton.*

FIG. 73b

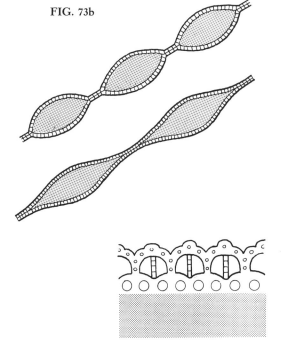

74a *Motif of Brussels tape overlaid with net and attached by stitches which are long on the reverse side and will be invisible on the face.*

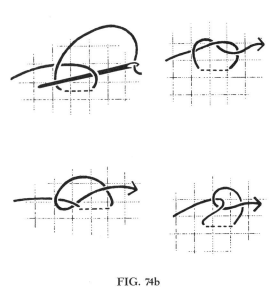

FIG. 74b

73b *Brussels Princess.* **Above** Leaf tapes. **Below** A petal tape enlarged.

74b *Two types of knot used to fix the stitches in position.*

Examples of tape-based laces

The names below do not appear in nineteenth-century writings, except for Luxeuil. Also, a large number of surviving laces incorporate a mixture of ideas which do not fit into any clearly-defined category.

Battenberg The bars are overcast, and the filling stitches are mainly point d'Alençon and backstitch wheels. The characteristic thick thread, broad tapes and slack designs of looped petal formations are effective from a distance, for example on table covers.

Branscombe On the outer side of each buttonhole-stitched bar is a single picot known as a pip (Italian, *pippiolini*) (fig. 71 a or b). Venetian edging is worked along the outer border of the lace. The fillings consist of about sixteen varieties of decorative buttonhole stitches.

Point de Milan Designs to some extent follow those of eighteenth-century Milanese bobbin laces. There is a mesh ground of tulle stitch (fig. 72a). The main filling stitch is the close form of detached buttonhole stitch with a straight return. Gaps are left between selected stitches to form diamond or other shaped patterns. Spaces within the flowers may be crossed by buttonhole-stitched bars each bearing a single short picot (fig. 71e). The outer picot border is knotted (fig. 71g).

Dichtl/Dickel A thick braid is curved into sinuous contortions forming an abstract design. The braids are linked by heavy buttonhole-stitched bars. There are seldom any filling stitches.

Ardenza This was made commercially in a restricted area near Leghorn, just south of Pisa, in the twentieth century, using a bobbin-made tape at first, which was later replaced by a machine-made one. The simple flower forms have delicate fillings of open detached buttonhole stitch with a straight return, while the scrolls are crossed by bars which are lightly buttonhole-stitched so that they look like Ladderwork. The ground bars are thin and overcast.

Luxeuil The tape is loosely twill-woven but has no holes along the edges, so that a pointed needle has to be used.

Vermicelli Thin braids looped like e's.

8
ARMENIAN

KNOTTED LACES form a relatively small group among the lace techniques. They include several distinct types:

Macramé is made from many threads suspended vertically and fastened together by a limited range of knots, such as the Solomon knot and the half hitch. The threads are manipulated by hand, though bobbins may be used as thread-holders to prevent tangling when the work is fine.

Filet is made from a very long single strand of thread. This is held on a shuttle and worked with a spacer to build up a miniaturized fishing net of equal-sized squares fixed by a fish-net knot at each corner. Alternatively a sheet-bend, or an overhand knot, or a square reef-knot are found in nineteenth-century filets. The knot can also be made with a needle, but then the length of thread is short and so inconvenient for constructing pieces of significant size.

Tatting also is worked with a single thread held on a shuttle, but without the gauge. Larkshead/ cow hitch/reversed half-hitch knots are used.

Macramé, filet and tatting must be excluded from this book because of the way they are made, and this chapter will be restricted to knotted laces traditionally made with a sewing needle.

◇DISTRIBUTION Needle-knotted laces are associated with the eastern Mediterranean, most especially Turkey, Syria, Greece, Palestine, Morocco, Tunisia, and the high valleys of Piedmont, north of Genoa. Some of the knots take their names from places such as Smyrna, Rodi and Armenia. Macramé itself is an Arabic word.

The technique was carried by the Moors to Spain where *redecillas* were made and used for bags and hair nets.

◇HISTORY Knotted laces are said to be of ancient origin dating back at least to the time of Nebuchadnezzar, around 600BC, when a wooden needle was used. However the market appears to have been entirely local until the late nineteenth century, and they were always well outside the mainstream of European fashion which, for almost 400 years, was dominated by the manufacturers of Flanders, France and Venice. Needle-knotted laces later became a tourist attraction, and the patterns were copied using a much quicker crochet technique.

◇STITCHES Knots differ from the detached and twisted buttonhole stitches in that the interlacing of threads ties them into positions which make movement impossible, except, perhaps, sideways along the support thread. This has the advantage that the fabric is strong and holds fast if damaged. However, it also has the double disadvantage that it makes the stitches of older laces extremely difficult to analyze, while mistakes in current manufacture are hard to alter. Beginners, therefore, beware: do not tighten the knots completely until you are quite certain that their position, and the loops of thread connecting them, are precisely as you want.

Several types of knot are found. They do not in themselves sharply differentiate specific forms, but, in combination with typical design styles, five distinct laces can be identified: Puncetto; Arab lace; Palestine lace; Armenian lace; and Bebilla.

The making of the four main types of knot will be described first; then the construction of the actual laces.

The Puncetto knot This is an overhand knot with half-hitch appearance. The stitches are worked very closely together in thick thread, and tightened so that the final impression on the face side is of a series of vertical bars. The knots are made in both directions, left-right and right-left, with the needle pointing away from you. On the reverse side it can be seen that the tilt of the knots is in opposite directions in successive rows. In the left-right row the tip of the knot slopes to the right, in the right-left row the slope is towards the left. The entry point of the thread is always at the base of the knot, and its exit from the top (fig. 75).

Exactly the same stitch is used in Arab laces, and the differences between Arab and Puncetto relate to spacing, design and geographical origin.

FIG. 75

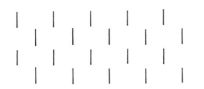 

75 *The appearance of Puncetto knots spaced out.* **Left** *Face side.* **Right** *Reverse.*

To make the stitch Fig. 76. Starting at the left, place the needle under the foundation cord, or under the loop of the previous row, then under the incoming thread, with the point away from you. Twist the thread around the needle as shown and tighten the twist. Pull the needle slowly through, guiding the threads with the thumb so that the stitch is not misplaced.

76 *Puncetto knots, face side.*

FIG. 76a

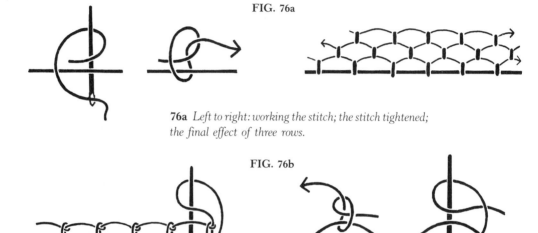

76a *Left to right: working the stitch; the stitch tightened; the final effect of three rows.*

FIG. 76b

76b *Working the knot from right to left.*

The Palestine knot/Nazareth stitch/Jewish knotting The overhand knot is worked in a slightly different manner (fig. 77a) so that it appears as a clear tie, not a vertical stroke. Like Puncetto, the direction of the knots is reversed in alternate rows (fig. 77b), but unlike Puncetto the lace looks the same on face and reverse sides. Decorative effects along the border of the lace are produced by arranging the knots in clusters, or by a limited use of other stitches such as the knotted buttonhole stitch (fig. 77c).

Opposite Halas lace. **Above** A fan leaf in coloured silks, designed by Árpád Dékáni, c.1906. The bodies of the birds are in darning stitch, the tails of radiating strands of thread caught by cross-linkages; the background of varied buttonhole stitches. **Below** Deer worked in white linen thread. In Dékáni's animals, the crisp formal symmetry of the French Art Nouveau is blurred by softened contours.

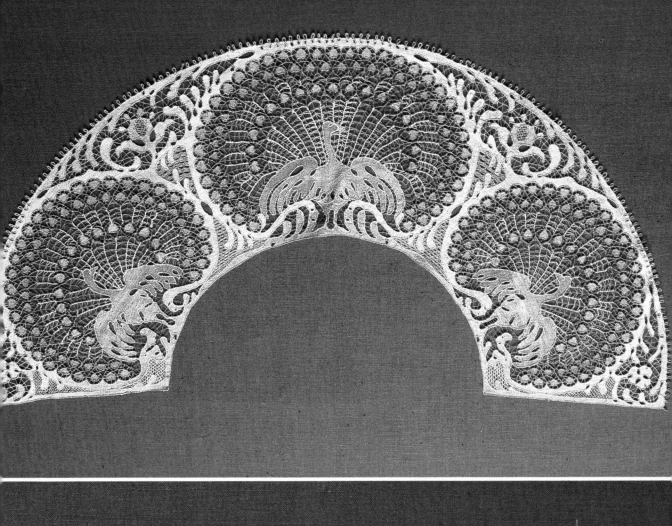
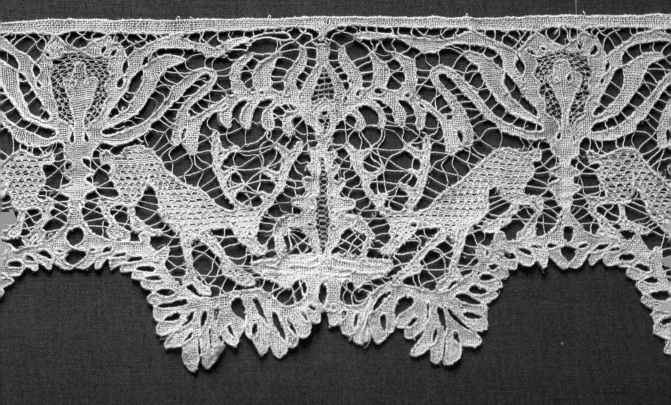

77 *Palestine knots.*

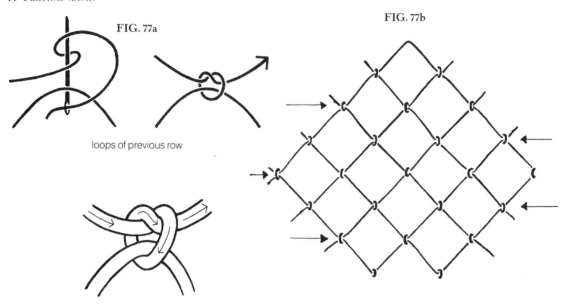

FIG. 77a

FIG. 77b

loops of previous row

77a *Left to right: working the stitch; the stitch tightened; the appearance in the actual knot, enlarged.*

77b *Sketch to show reversal of knots in alternate rows, either face or reverse side. The arrows indicate the direction of working. Loops are left between the knots so that the final effect is of a diamond-shaped network.*

FIG. 77c

77c *The knotted buttonhole stitch: make a detached buttonhole stitch (see fig. 31, page 39), take the needle under the crossed loops and tighten the knot, leaving a broad loop below.*

Opposite Tape-based laces. **Above** 'Honiton point' being worked over blue calico and showing the string-of-sausages appearance of 'Honiton tape'; Vermicelli lace – narrow braid is looped into a delicate design. **Below** Princess lace, shaped tapes are appliquéd onto net; Branscombe-type lace, the border of the entire design is edged with Venetian picots; Dichtl lace, there is no buttonhole-stitching except for the saw-toothed bars.

The Armenian knot (also known as Smyrna or Rodi). This is a larger knot than either the Puncetto or the Palestine. Also, unlike them, although the knots are made along the lace in a left-right direction, and then back again from right to left, every row appears the same, in the tilt of the knots and in the entry and exit slopes of the threads (fig. 78a). This is achieved by working left-right rows in the normal manner with the needle pointing away from you (fig.78b), but in right-left rows turn the needle towards you and reverse the twist of the threads (fig. 78c). Rarely, in small areas of the lace, every other row of knots is replaced by a straight return thread.

Note Rodi and Smyrna are ambiguous names and some of the stitches they are applied to do not appear in Armenian laces at all.

78 *Armenian knot.*

FIG. 78b

FIG. 78c

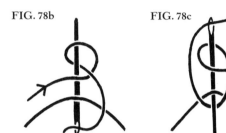

FIG. 78a

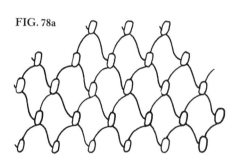

78b *The left-right way of making the knot. As in other needle-knotted laces, the entry point of the thread is lower than its exit.*

78c *The right-left way of making the knot. The entry point of the thread is higher than its exit. The shape of the loops and the slope of the knots is identical in every stitch, and it is impossible to tell in which direction any particular row has been worked.*

78a *The general appearance of the lace. Every knot and loop is identical. Here, the tip tilts to the right, which normally indicates a left-right direction of working. The other side of the lace would look the same except that all the knots slope in the reverse direction, with the tip towards the left.*

FIG. 78d

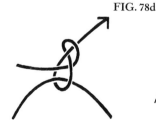

78d *The knot in actual laces: as the twists of thread slide over each other, the set of the knot changes and several slightly different appearances are presented.*

The Bebilla knot This is a larger and more complex stitch than the Armenian knot. It is worked in the right-left direction only, and the thread is carried back from left to right as a straight return. Thus all the knots slope in the same direction, the tip towards the left. The direction of working is clearly visible in the actual lace where the reverse side is indicated by the back of the flower heads and, less obviously, by thread joins. This stitch is described in detail in the Bebilla project (see figs. 84 and 85). A slightly different stitch, named by Tashjian as 'Armenian stitch' is used to cover the horsehair which represents the earth in the pattern which will be described (fig. 90). As already indicated, confusion of names is frequent and complex – but so it is for non-knotted lace stitches and for non-needle-lace knots.

◇MATERIALS   Cotton or linen thread, used for Puncetto, Arab lace and Palestine lace, should be strong, well-twisted, smooth, non-fluffy and relatively thick. For Armenian lace and Bebilla, a loosely-spun silk of either a creamy ivory colour or dyed in brilliantly contrasting shades, is traditionally used.

A blunt tipped needle.

A support such as a polystyrene block, firm enough to take pins.

For Bebilla, horsehair and/or fine wire.

◇THE LACES   Puncetto, Arab and Armenian laces are all to some extent a throwback to Antique Cutworks, most notably in the geometric form of the design and in the absence of any structured ground.

The laces are not worked over a drawn or printed pattern. A large-scale stitch plan can be followed, but it is more usual to copy an actual piece of lace or, for the literate – and many of the nineteenth- and early twentieth-century workers were not – directions are written out in terms of loops missed, loops enlarged, stitches added and so forth. This necessitates counting.

FIG. 79

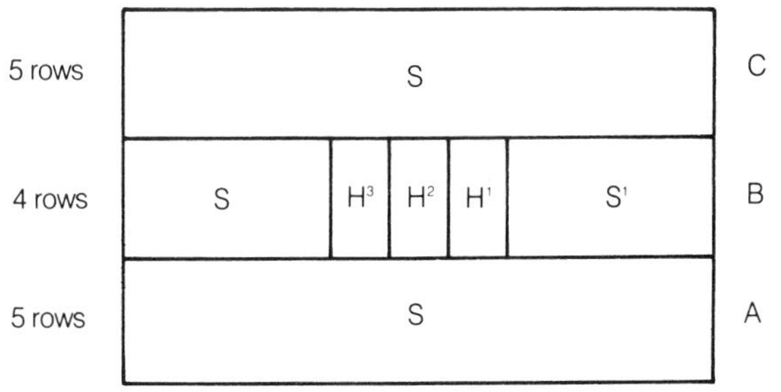

5 rows	S		C
4 rows	S	H³ H² H¹ S¹	B
5 rows	S		A

79 *A simple pattern for Puncetto.*
S = solid areas
H = holes

Puncetto

The starting point can be the hem of a cloth or, if the lace is to be worked as an isolated strip, a foundation cord.

Stretch a cord from right to left, widthways of the lace. Work a full row of knots as described on page 88, placing them very close together so that there will just be room for the stitches of row 2 to fit between them. For practice, a very simple design is given (fig. 79). This can be repeated as often as necessary to make, for example, a bookmark.

Block A Row 1: work twenty-three stitches from left to right over the foundation cord. Row 2: work back from right to left, taking the needle under the loops of row 1. Repeat rows 1, 2 and 1 again, ending at the right-hand side.

Block B Row 6: work six Puncetto stitches. Repeat this row four times, ending at the left-hand side of S^1. Miss two loops, then work one stitch, but leave enough thread to outline a small square . Hold the thread in position at X and Y, then work one Puncetto stitch as shown (fig. 80a). Work upwards along the side of the square, making six stitches very close together (fig 80b). This forms a column. At the top, take the thread across and down to form two sides of the next square. Proceed as before. Make a third square, but do not work a column (fig. 80c). Work six knots across to the left side of the lace. Work four more rows of six stitches. This brings you to the same level as the top of the squares.

Block C Work five rows of Puncetto stitches right across the lace. Finish off the thread. Or repeat B and C.

Decorative picots can be added along the border in a manner similar to the ring picot used in buttonhole stitch laces (fig. 71f, page 82). Take the thread back in a small arc over three stitches. Work Puncetto knots over the arc, back to the starting point (fig. 80d).

The dense texturing of Puncetto work can be seen in the photograph on page 106.

80 *Puncetto lace.*

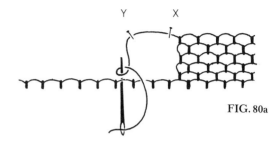

80a *The outline of the first square (H^1).*

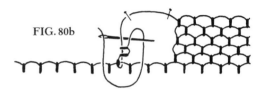

80b *Working Puncetto knots along the side.*

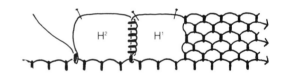

80c *The outline of the second square (H^2).*

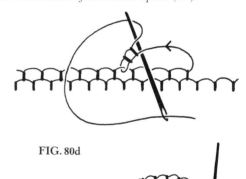

FIG. 80d

80d *A ring picot oversewn with Puncetto knots.*

Arab lace

The Puncetto knot is used, but the stitches are spaced more widely apart in both a horizontal and vertical direction so that the connecting loops are clearly seen. The designs are rigidly formal and the work is supported along the sides by foundation cords made of chain-stitching. Edgings are worked widthways, as in Puncetto. Usually both borders are straight. Use a fairly long thread, about 2 m (2 yd). Twist it a little between stitches to prevent it becoming too curly.

The pattern

A simple design is shown in fig. 81. It consists basically of either working a knot in every loop of the previous row, or in missing two, three or four loops, then making up that number again in the next row, so that a slit-like hole is created.

Written directions for the pattern may be off-putting. For example:
Row 1: one stitch, miss two loops, one stitch, miss two loops.
Row 2: six stitches, filling in the two missed (twice) to make the holes.

Row 3: miss two loops, one stitch, miss two loops, one stitch.
Row 4: six stitches... and so on for thirty rows, or however long the repeat may be.

It is simpler to work from a large scale diagram, an actual piece of lace, or a very clear photograph.

Palestine lace

Edgings are worked lengthwise over a foundation cord. This is a very open and stringy lace, looking in its mesh-like form strikingly similar to filet. However the meshes are diamond-shaped instead of straight-on square; and the designs, restricted to the border, are made by clustered stitches with loops extended to encompass spaces, giving the impression of a series of half-open fans (fig.82). In filet, by contrast, the stitches are always evenly spaced and their arrangement plays no part in the design, which is entirely dependent on added running or darning stitches.

FIG. 82

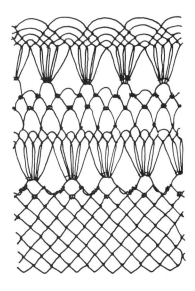

FIG. 81

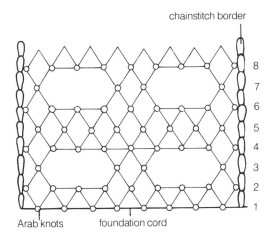

chainstitch border

Arab knots   foundation cord

81 *Design for an Arab lace. 1–8 rows = in the order of working. Rows 1, 3, 5 and 7 are worked from left-right, and rows 2, 4, 6 and 8, right-left.*

82 *Palestine lace showing how groupings of stitches and adjustments of loop size can produce a decorative effect.*

83 *Armenian lace.*

FIG. 83a

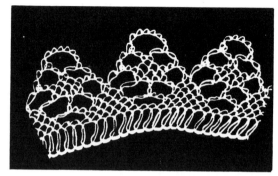

FIG. 83b

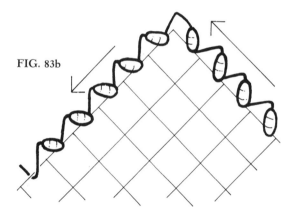

FIG. 83c

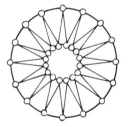

83a and b *Armenian lace showing diagonal bands and triangles which form the pattern. Both edgings have dentate borders as in 83b. The lace above has additional hoops worked along the foundation cord (see fig. 90, page 100).*

83c *Armenian 'wheels'. The use of such wheels in an actual lace can be seen in the collar to the left in the photograph on page 109. Armenian wheels may be linked via a Moorish influence with the Teneriffe wheels or rosettes described on page 110 (fig. 97). However, the knots are different – Armenian in one, overhand in the other; and so is the mode of construction. Teneriffe is based on a skeleton of fixed diameters, while Armenian is worked freehand, the knots being linked only to each other.*

Armenian lace

This is used to make circular table mats, beginning with a tiny circle and working outwards; or to border towel ends, handkerchiefs, etc., taking the first row of stitches into the edge of the cloth; or as a strip with a dentate border, beginning over a foundation cord stretched lengthwise of the lace.

Work the stitch illustrated in fig. 78. Acute loops are left between each knot, spacing them out. Decorative triangular shaped areas can be constructed by decreasing one stitch at the beginning and end of each row. A firm straight edge is then given to the triangle by pulling the loops more tightly at the sides. Diagonal bands within the lace can be worked similarly (fig. 83a).

The foundation cord may have a row of hoops added to its lower side as in Bebilla (see fig. 90). An additional row of 'teeth' may be added to a dentate border by a single row of Armenian knots with sharply asymmetrical loops (fig. 83b).

To make Armenian 'wheels'

Make a small ring of thread. Work a series of Armenian knots along it, leaving long loops between adjacent knots. When you have enough loops, for example seventeen, pull the central ring of thread to bring them more closely together, and knot the two ends firmly. Carry a thread around the outer tip of the loops and tie loops and thread together by a series of an equal number of Armenian knots, in this case seventeen. If desired, triangular loops can be left between these knots, and the wheel extended outwards by several similar rows (fig. 83c).

Bebilla

Bebilla is a three-dimensional lace of small flowers made to stand independently along a narrow border which represents the brown earth and green grass mounds. Traditionally, silks vividly coloured with vegetable dyes in shades of scarlet, emerald, canary yellow, terra cotta and black were used, imitating the glowing colours of a garden in full bloom.

Unlike the other needle-knotted laces, Bebilla stitches are worked in one direction only, alternating with a straight return thread. This gives the

FIG. 84

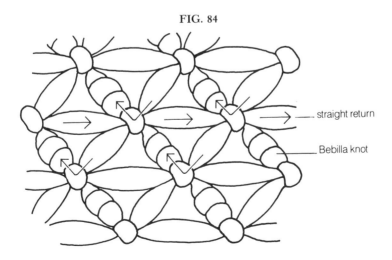

straight return

Bebilla knot

84 *Detail of Bebilla lace stitches. The arrows show the direction of working.*

85 *Stages in making the Bebilla knot.*

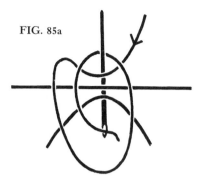

FIG. 85a

FIG. 85b

85a *Take the needle under the loop of the previous row, under the return thread and under the incoming thread. Loop the thread nearest to the eye of the needle under the needle from left to right.*

85b *Wind the incoming thread over the needle from left to right and back under from right to left.*

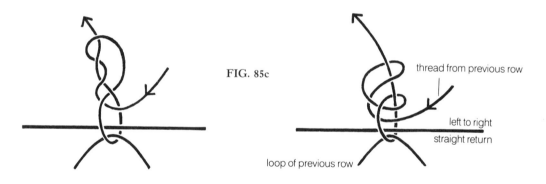

FIG. 85c

thread from previous row

left to right
straight return

loop of previous row

85c *Tighten the knot. As you do this the threads will slip over each other, presenting a variety of appearances.*

lace a peculiar starry quality, enhanced by the loosely-twisted glossy silk which swells out in the loops and then is abruptly narrowed as the knot constricts it (fig. 84). In fact the knots are tied so tightly that the precise course of the thread is difficult to follow.

According to Ionides, who collected a wide range of Bebilla examples, the knot is made from left to right, but this appears from actual laces to be incorrect. The directions for making are shown in fig. 85 .

The design

In Bebilla the design does not depend on variable spacings of stitches as it does in the other needle-knotted laces. On the contrary, it is of the utmost importance that all the stitches and loops are of equal size, and that all the knots are centrally placed. Shaped pieces are built up and then fitted together to make buds, leaves, stem bases and flowers (figs. 86-92).

The earth Stretch a straight length of horsehair to form the base. Using brown thread, and start-

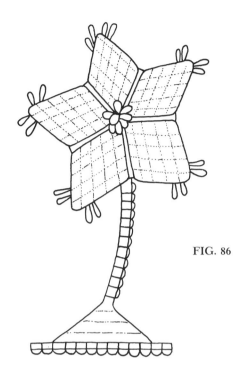

FIG. 86

86 *A Bebilla flower.*

ing at the right-hand side with the needle pointing away from you, make a row of Bebilla knots fairly close together using the horsehair as a foundation cord. Leave shallow loops between the knots so that the finished row presents a tooth-like appearance. (fig. 87).

Stem base In the middle part of the 'earth', work a triangle in light green silk. Row 1: starting at the right side, work five Bebilla knots with angular loops between. Row 2: carry the thread straight back to the right-hand side. Row 3: work four knots into the loops of row 1, taking in the return thread also. Row 4: as row 2. Row 5: work three knots into the loops of row 3. Catch the last knot back to the previous stitch, and fasten off the thread (fig. 88).

FIG. 87

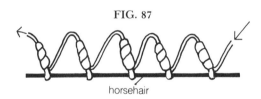

horsehair

87 *The first row of the stem base.*

FIG. 88

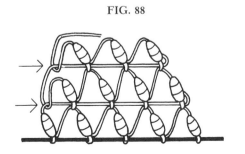

88 *A sketch to show the stitch arrangement in the stem base.*

FIG. 89

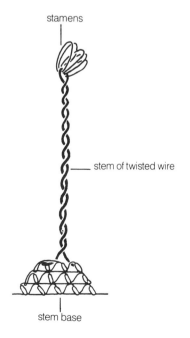

stamens

stem of twisted wire

stem base

89 *The flower stalk.*

The stem Wrap a thin wire around with green silk. Pass one end of the wire through the upper loops of the stem base, bend it over at the top, halfway along its length, and wind strands of gold silk in a loose circle round and round the loop so formed. These will make the stamens at the centre of the flower. Tighten the wire loop to hold them firmly, then carry the wire back to the stem base, twisting the two parts round each other as you go (fig. 89). To give the stem additional width, work a single row of knotted stitches along it. In actual laces these correspond exactly with Tashjian's 'Armenian stitch'. Turn the work so that the lower end of the stem is to the right-hand side. Then, beginning at the right, with the needle pointed away from you take it under the wire stem and under the incoming thread; loop the thread nearest to the eye under the needle from right to left, over from left to right and under from right to left; pull the needle through (fig. 90a). As usual the finished stitch is slightly asymmetrical, the incoming thread being lower than the outgoing one (fig. 90b). Now knot these two threads together as shown (fig. 90c). Continue in this way all along the stem. The result will be a series of even hoops (fig. 90d).

90 *'Armenian stitch' used to make the hoops along the flower stalk.*

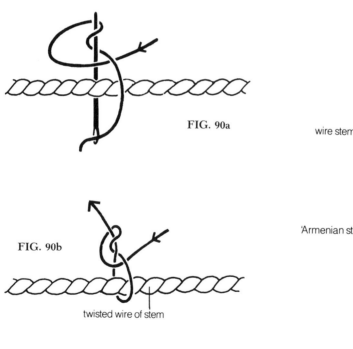

FIG. 90a

FIG. 90b

twisted wire of stem

FIG. 90c

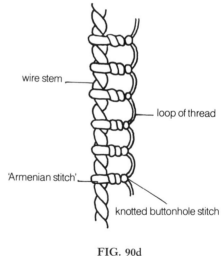

wire stem

loop of thread

'Armenian stitch'

knotted buttonhole stitch

FIG. 90d

90a *The dotted line indicates the greater length of the thread.*
90b *The asymmetrical entry and exit point of the thread.*
90c *Making a knotted buttonhole stitch to fix the two loop threads at the same height.*
90d *Diagram to show the hoops along the stem.*

FIG. 91

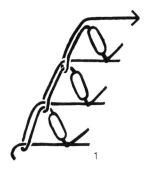

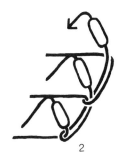

Petals These are worked in a similar manner to the stem base, increasing then decreasing the number of stitches per row (fig. 91). The sides can be strengthened by linking the threads together at either end of each row as it is worked, but it might be simpler to make a diamond-shaped frame of thin wire and loop the threads over this.

The tips of the petals can be decorated with tufts of picots by working additional Bebilla stitches at the ends of the rows (see fig. 86), holding the loops outwards with pins so that they are longer than usual. Alternatively a dentate border in a different colour can be added (fig. 92).

In professional work the petals are made as a single unit by working a circle of Bebilla knots tightly around the loop of the stem wire, then continuing outwards to make five separate petals. For a beginner, however, it is much simpler to make the petals one at a time and then stitch them together.

To complete the earth Turn the lace so that the horsehair is at the top. With the needle pointing away from you make a row of 'Armenian stitches' from right to left between the brown earth stitches first worked (see fig. 87). Now knot the loops together, as described in fig. 90. If preferred, this row of 'Armenian stitches' can be worked before the rest of the flower is begun.

91 *The arrangement of stitches in a petal. The thicker lines represent Bebilla knots.*
(1) Linking the rows as the stitches decrease: carry the thread from the top of the last stitch down over the previous row's end loop, then go up again to begin the left-right straight return.
(2) Linking the rows together as the number of stitches is increased: carry the left-right straight return down to the previous row, link over the threads, go up again and commence the knot row.

FIG. 92

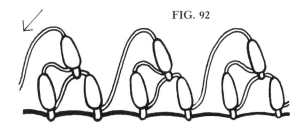

92 *A separate dentate border added to a petal or leaf. Work Bebilla knots one and two, leaving a normal loop between. Take the outgoing thread from two back to the right. Work stitch three over the loop between one and two. Carry the thread from three down to the petal. Repeat this set of thread movements throughout the border trim.*

9
TENERIFFE

*H*OWEVER different from each other the various needle-made laces may appear, the use of a needle and a single thread is not the only thing which links them together. A complex network of relationships can be traced as if some subtle evolutionary force was at work, branching off designs and techniques then reassembling them into apparently new forms, so that none is completely isolated. Teneriffe laces are geometric in design and, except that their units are essentially circular rather than square, the arrangement of diagonals, curves and angles is similar to Antique Cutwork and Reticella (Chapters 2 and 3). The delicate circles found in some Armenian/Bebilla laces are reminiscent of silky spider webs; at the same time Teneriffe laces use the overhand knot, which is a minor but essential part of knotted lace design (Chapter 8).

◇THE NAME   'Teneriffe' is only one of a group of laces that have in common an arrangement of threads radiating from a central point towards a circular outline, like spokes radiating from the hub of a wheel. Naturally enough, a general name for these laces is 'wheel' laces. This is expressed by the Spanish term *Ruedas*, meaning a wheel or circle. The varieties of ruedas have distinguishing names, such as *Sol* (Spanish, meaning sun) lace where the decoration of the spokes curves outwards from the centre like tongues of flame or a fiery sunburst.

Other names are *Ñanduti*, meaning spider's web, a lace of fragile silk for which 'wheel' alone would be too hefty a simile and *Tucuman* and *Teneriffe* which are place names.

◇DISTRIBUTION   Wheel laces are associated with areas which are, or were, under Spanish or Portuguese influence, most especially Spain, South America, Mexico and the Canary Islands. The name Ruedas is associated with Spain, Ñanduti with Paraguay, Sol with Brazil, Tucuman with Argentina, and Teneriffe with the Canary Islands. They are distinguished not only geographically, but by some features of technique and design.

◇HISTORY   Although wheel laces are known from sixteenth-century Spain, most of the surviving examples date from the mid-nineteenth century or later. The oldest laces were probably ecclesiastical. In the early nineteenth century, making Ñanduti was a drawing-room pastime for the leisured ladies of Paraguay, using fine cotton or thread made of pineapple fibres. But it suffered the fate of other handmade laces, becoming coarser, simpler, less time-consuming, and tourist-orientated. By the early twentieth century, in the lace-making centre of Itaugua, nearly every family in the village, some 1,000 women aged anywhere from nine to ninety, were occupied exclusively with making Ñanduti for pillow shams, curtains, gowns and all sorts of fashion accessories. Harper's Bazar in 1903 introduced it as a 'new lace' which had sprung into favour as a 'decidedly utilitarian diversion for gentlewomen... while not usurping the Battenberg and Renaissance laces [Chapter 7] which have already come in for their share of patronage.'

◇STITCHES There are only two main stitches, needleweaving and overhand knots, and it is amazing the variety of decorative effects which can be achieved in this simple manner. There are fifty or more altogether, and each is known by name; for example, passion flower, joined ant-hills, parrot's beak, small bush whose flower sticks to whatever touches it [some kind of burr?], flock of sheep and fish ribs. The number of such designs in common use dwindled, until by the early twentieth century, eleven or twelve together in one piece of lace was regarded as high quality. Even then the work was slow. Figures quoted in 1909 give two months' steady labour, working from sunrise to sunset, as the necessary time to produce one fine handkerchief; while a bolero (or *torero*) took four to six months, and a parasol cover more than a year.

◇MATERIALS A long blunt-tipped needle, slightly curved and flattened at the tip, to enable it to pass more easily through the web.

Fine white cotton or corn-coloured silk were traditional, but there is no reason why thicker, dyed, threads should not be used for trying out the technique.

A pattern, and some kind of support such as a small cushion.

Strong pins about 3 cm ($1\frac{1}{4}$ in) long.

The pattern

Fig. 93 shows a simple decoration which is fairly near to the Ñanduti 'fish rib' pattern. Keep this beside you; it is not easy to follow the design if it is placed entirely beneath the work. The lace design is made by weaving the needle in and out

of a variable number of radii, and by knotting the radii together in variable clusters.

Laying the web

The following method is not entirely a traditional one, but it is very simple. Its object is to avoid

FIG. 93

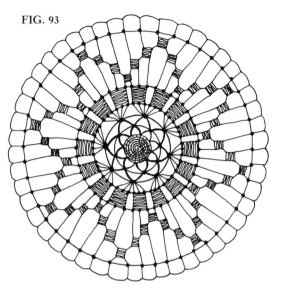

93 *Pattern for spider-web lace. The forty-eight radii cannot be shown in detail in the centre, but all the knot circles have been marked.*

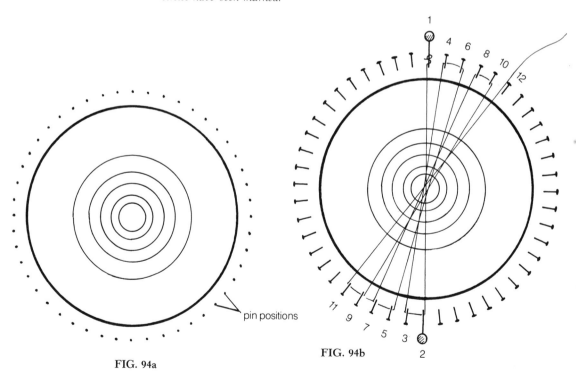

pin positions

FIG. 94a

FIG. 94b

94a *Guide lines for the circles and for the pin positions which mark the ends of the diameters.*

94b *The first diameters put in. The threads have been spaced to show how they pass behind the pins. This spreads the threads more than would happen in the actual work where they would be pulled taut across the centre.*

the tedium of drawing precisely accurate circles and precisely placed diameters in pencil on cloth, by using ready-made ones. In the past, cloths ready-printed with Teneriffe designs could be bought .

Trace or photocopy the outline shown in fig. 94a onto a firm translucent paper. Lay this over a small cushion (about 11 cm [$4\frac{1}{2}$ in] square) which has been covered with a blue or dark green cloth so that the threads will show up clearly. Place pins around the outside at every point where circle and diameters intersect. The pins will support the threads during working and so they must be firmly fixed in the cushion with the heads slanting outwards. Mark the opposite ends of one diameter with two pins which are larger and have differently coloured heads from the rest. This helps to locate precisely opposite points and also marks the starting position for later concentric circles.

Use a ball of thread so that you can go the whole way round without any joins being necessary. First tie the thread with a small knot to one of the coloured pins. Take it across the centre and loop it over the opposite pin; then over the one next to it to the left. Take the thread back across the centre and loop it over its opposite pin and the one next to it to the right. Proceed in this way until all the diameters have been put in, ending at the point where you started.

All the threads must cross at the centre (fig. 94b). Neatly tie the ending thread to the starting thread in the central area so that it will be hidden by later work. Take a long end of thread, about a metre (a yard), thread the needle again, and you are ready to begin the design.

Adding the design to the web

1 Starting at the centre take the needle over and under the radii. Back-stitch darning, also known as rib stitch (fig. 95a) gives a much firmer and neater appearance than ordinary darning (fig. 95b). Work several times around the central area in this manner, moving consistently in an anti-

FIG. 95a

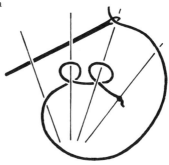

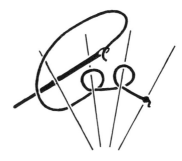

FIG. 95b

starting point

95a *Stage 1. Working rib stitch in two movements, under two radii then back over one of them.*
95b *Darning stitch: when there is an even number of radii two must be taken together or the stitches will not alternate. Spaced out, as shown here, this move is very obvious, but working over forty-eight closely set threads it would never be noticed.*

FIG. 95c

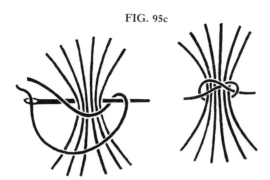

95c *The overhand knot. Adjust the thread so that the knot is correctly positioned, hold it down with the thumb and draw the needle through slowly.*

clockwise direction. Pack the stitches in tightly with the tip of the needle.

2 Then tie the radii together in groups of six using the overhand knot (fig. 95c). Total eight knots. Work over the innermost circle in fig. 94 so that each knot is at precisely the same distance from the centre of the circle.

3 At the next circle, tie three radii from one group to three of the next group, and so on all the way round (fig. 95d). Total eight knots.

4 Work forty-eight knots, one on each radius, spacing them evenly the whole way round (fig. 95d).

5 Take the radii in groups of three, splitting the six strands of stage (3) into two blocks. Weave the needle over and under within each three-thread group four times, working outwards from the centre. Pull the threads fairly tightly so that the blocks become square instead of triangular. After completing block 1, carry the thread across

FIG. 95d

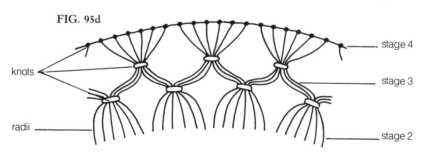

95d *Stages 2, 3 and 4.*

Opposite Knotted laces, nineteenth and twentieth centuries. **Clockwise from top right** Puncetto with fragments of Arab lace on either side; a garland of Bebilla flowers in coloured silks; Palestine lace, the design made by knotting threads into groups; a Reticella design imitated by Puncetto,; a child's bib in Armenian lace, with rosettes of petals worked in Bebilla stitch; silk Armenian collar made of wheels laid around flowers; Puncetto simulating Antique Cutwork and Punto in aria; a torchon-like edge of Armenian knotting.

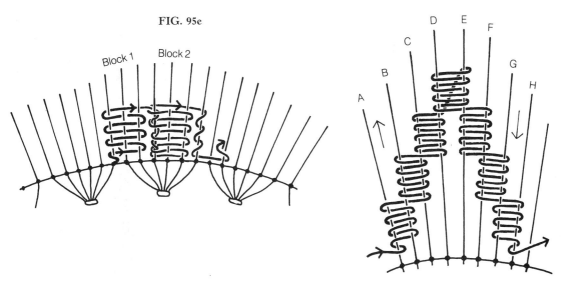

FIG. 95e

FIG. 95f

95e *Stage 5.*
95f *Stages 7 and 8. The threads are shown spaced out to make the stitches clearer.*
In practice the little blocks of needleweaving draw the pairs of radii close together
(see fig.93).

to block 2, and overcast down the outer radius. Work the second block, moving upwards (fig. 95e). The needleweaving will cover the overcast stitches. Carry the thread across to block 3 and continue in this way until all sixteen blocks are completed.

6 Work another forty-eight knots, one on each radius, evenly spaced.

7 Now take the radii in groups of two. Begin with A and B in fig. 95f, and needleweave for four rows. At the top, take B and C together for four rows, then C and D for four rows, continuing to work outwards all the time. Finally take D and E together.

8 Now climb down again, taking the thread through the back of the DE block. E and F are worked on a level with C and D; F and G on a level with B and C; and G and H on a level with A and B. Continue in this manner over the remaining radii. This will produce eight complete fish ribs in all.

9 Tuck the thread end into the reverse side of the centre (the hub of the wheel, the spider in its web). Now fix the thread by a knot to one of the radii as near the circumference of the circle as possible. Tie a further forty-eight knots, linking all the radii together at equal intervals, the final knot coinciding with the first.

10 The wheel is now finished. Remove it from its cushion by taking out the pins.

Opposite Wheel laces. **Centre** A fan leaf of Nañduti in corn-coloured silk on bone sticks. **Left** A mantilla and handkerchief of similar work but with more varied designs (Paraguay, nineteenth century). **Right and left centre** An insertion of ruedas combined with Cutwork and needleweaving; Reticella-style ruedas, the triangles needlewoven instead of buttonhole-stitched; a double square of dense ruedas in sunburst form. All Spanish, seventeenth century. **Centre right** Working wheel-lace within a circle of cut-out fabric; a small mat of Mexican drawnwork.

To make more spider-web circles

Spider-web circles are very rarely more than 6 cm (2½ in) across, and are often no more than 4 cm (1½ in). They are never individually enlarged to form appreciable mats, as happens in the Puncetto and Armenian laces. Large pieces of lace, therefore, can only be constructed by joining several small pieces together.

In Teneriffe lace the circles are called 'rosettes'. A labour-saving way of making a number of them is to use the same pin set-up for each. When the first rosette is finished, do not remove it, but cover it with a piece of paper, leaving all the pins still showing. Work a second separate rosette over the first, finish it off, cover with paper, and work a third rosette over the second. It may be necessary to raise the pins a little to accommodate the new sets of diameters, but if the pins are sufficiently long some twelve rosettes can be made in this way before the pins become unstable. Even when the pins and rosettes are finally removed, the pins can at once be replaced in the same holes, and the factory-like procedure continued.

It is not necessary for every rosette to be identical. In theory at least, each could have a different pattern – provided that they are all based around

twenty-four diameters. Once the basic technique of making spider-web laces is mastered, any actual piece of lace, or any clearly drawn pattern, can be copied quite easlily.

The completed rosettes are arranged in position and stitched together where their sides touch, simply by taking a thread in and out of adjacent loops (fig. 96).

Variations

Rosettes of the early twentieth century
Under pressure to produce greater quantities more quickly and more cheaply, the labour-intensive Ñanduti wheels were often replaced by the simplest possible constructions.

Example Make twenty-four diameters as before (see fig. 94). Work rib stitch for several rows. Fasten the thread with a small knot, then carry it up about 6 mm ($\frac{3}{16}$ in) and make a circle of overhand knots, holding two radii together with each knot. Take the thread up again until it is near the pins. Work a second circle of knots, catching together the right and left radii of adjacent pairs (fig. 97). Release the lace. The result bears a striking similarity to Armenian circles.

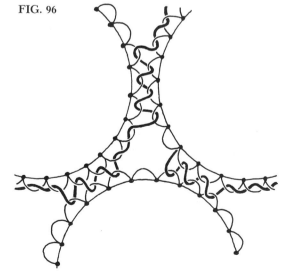

96 *The touching sides of three rosettes linked by stitches through their outer borders.*
97 *The formation of a simple wheel. The number of diameters is reduced.*

Mexican drawnwork

This resembles spider-web lace in the presence of simple circles similar to those described above. A finely woven cloth of silk has thread drawn in both directions to form openings of, for example, 1 cm ($\frac{6}{16}$ in) square, separated at the sides by three strands of wavy warps and wefts, and at the corners by small blocks of the original weave. Every open square is crossed by eight diameters. In one square a small darned central area is surrounded by two spaced rings of overhand knots. Alternating with these circles throughout the lace are needlewoven blocks in the form of a cross. The squares are linked by four threads passing right, left, upwards and downwards from the sixteen radii, and knotting the warps and wefts together into three strands before continuing to make the diameters of the needlewoven squares (fig. 98). The cutting of warps and wefts is restricted to the margin of the lace, which is closely oversewn.

Working on such a minute scale must have been a great strain for the eyes. Florence May refers to a dress of Mexican drawnwork which took 300 women nine years to complete. On a much coarser scale strips of insertion can be worked into table or bed covers using a thick cotton thread.

Alternative methods of laying the web

For the pattern shown on page 104, pins were used to support the diameters. The putting in of pins is simple, and the same arrangement can be used for many pieces, but they do have one major disadvantage. Once the diameters have been made, the pins must be pushed completely down into the cushion so that only their heads show, otherwise the thread will constantly catch on them as the decorative work is added. Three alternative methods are given below.

◇ The circle and diameter positions are marked on firm card, or photocopied and laid on to card. Instead of pins, loops of thread are used to provide support. This involves extra work in setting up the diameters since stitches have to be worked around the outermost circle, each stitch being large enough to accommodate two radii (fig. 99). Run stitches can be used, but back stitches give

FIG. 98

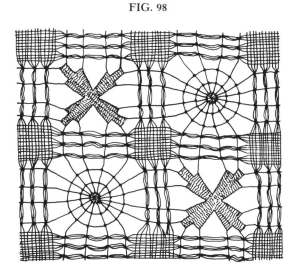

98 *Mexican drawnwork showing the alternation of knotted circles with needleweaving in the form of a cross. The residual warps and wefts are wavy.*

FIG. 99

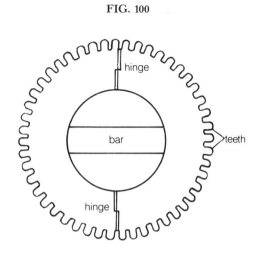

FIG. 100

99 *Run or back stitches to support the diameters, which are threaded through them.*

100 *Metal frame with serrated edge. To make the diameters the thread is wound over the teeth in just the same way as over pins. The bar holds the frame in position until the lace rosette is ready to be released.*

a much firmer anchorage. By this method it is less easy to use a continuous thread because of the bulk required. In coarser work a sufficient length of thread can be wound on a thin shuttle or netting needle which is then passed through each supporting stitch and back again. With small, fine work enough thread may be held on a needle. When the rosette is finished, cut through the supporting stitches from the back and lift the lace off the card.

◇ In the early twentieth century, metal frames with serrated edges were marketed (fig. 100). The thread was passed behind each tooth, as around two pins, following the same sequence and making sure that all the threads crossed near the centre. When the design was completed, the metal frame could be folded over so that the diameter threads were slack and easily lifted over the teeth.

◇ The rosettes can also be worked as an insertion within a cloth held in a wooden frame. The outline of the circles is drawn in pencil or charcoal onto cotton, linen or silk, and the end positions of the diameters marked. Alternatively a photocopy or drawing on paper can be placed on the cloth in the position required and the work done over it. This is scarcely traditional, but it is easy. The diameters are then put in in much the same way as for the first variation, but using the warps and wefts of the cloth in place of supporting stitches.

In this method it is impossible to use a continuous thread since only a sharp needle can be passed through the woven fabric. Once the diameters are complete, the design is worked using a blunt needle.

When the rosette is finished, turn the work to the reverse side, and cut away the cloth behind the lace. If a separate pattern has been used, remove it now. Working from the reverse side, stretch a cord along the outer ends of the diameters and roll the raw edge over this cord. Overcast this hem, catching the thread to the back of the supporting stitches, to prevent fraying during use. The overcasting stitches will be almost invisible from the front.

10
BURATTO

◇◇◇

*T*HE ITALIAN word *buratto* means a sieve, such as that used for flour, and it is an appropriate description of the square-meshed gauze fabric which forms the foundation of this type of embroidered lace. In the gauze weave, paired warps cross each other at each pick, encircling the weft and locking it in position (fig. 101).

The French term *lacis* is sometimes used for Buratto, and sometimes as a generic term for both Buratto and filet. These two laces have in common square meshes which are pre-made, one by weaving, the other by knotting. In both, the meshes form a basis for the addition of solid areas of design by running stitches worked either horizontally and/or vertically to make a darning stitch.

FIG. 101a

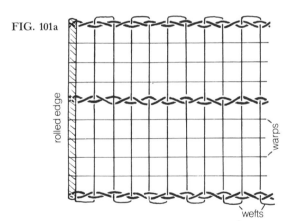

rolled edge

warps

wefts

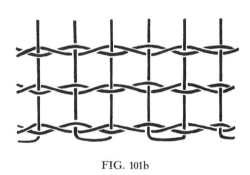

FIG. 101b

101a *A typical Buratto strip. The warps run lengthwise of the lace and cross around spaced wefts, which form a border of shallow looping along either edge. The beginning of the strip is rolled under. Crossed warps are shown in three rows only.*

101b *Detail showing the crossing of the warps to make the square-meshed gauze, and the loops formed by the wefts curving back into the fabric at the end of each pick.*

◇DISTRIBUTION The term Buratto suggests an Italian origin. Examples are also attributed to Spain, Sicily and Sardinia, but the areas of production were very restricted. A portrait of Catherine of Braganza by Stoop shows her wearing a collar of what appears to be Buratto lace around her shoulders. It was probably painted around 1660, before she left Portugal, to travel to England as the wife of Charles II.

◇HISTORY   Seventeeth-century Burattos survive, but in remarkably small numbers compared with other laces of that period. The gauze weave might be of white linen embroidered with white, or of silk dyed for example a rich brown and embroidered with softly glowing silks in many varied shades of green, blue, fawn, carnation and gold. The strips were straight-edged, often not more than 12 cm (4 $\frac{11}{16}$ in) wide. The warps ran lengthwise, and a small table loom could have been used. Far more rarely, the warps ran crosswise of the lace (fig. 102). This has two disadvantages: a much larger number of warps must be used, thus increasing the work of manipulating their crossings; and the long edges on both sides would have to be neatened after the gauze was taken from the loom.

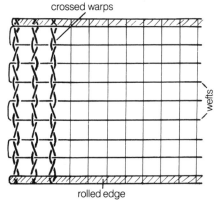

FIG. 102a

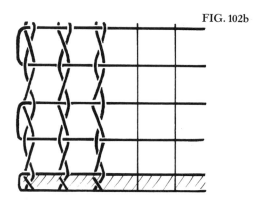

FIG. 102b

102a *A rare Buratto strip with the warps arranged across the short axis of the lace. The weft loops will then occur at either end, while the two long borders are rolled under and stitched.*
102b *Detail.*

Sixteenth- or seventeenth-century pattern books specifically for Burato (the Venetian spelling) are rare, but in fact any of the designs allocated to Drawnwork, filet, or 'counted thread work' could be used. As late as 1916, antique-type Burattos were still being made by Italian peasants, using hand-spun and hand-woven linen. Instructions appeared during the nineteenth century in Dillmont under the title 'netting'. She describes it as an imitation filet worked on 'net-canvas', which she also calls 'lacis', to save the 'lengthy and tedious task' of constructing the knotted ground. The 'net-canvas' is said to be supple, and she recommends a soft floss flax or Persian silk for the embroidery. Her designs do not follow traditional seventeenth-century Buratto forms but aim more to copy either nineteenth-century filets with their patterns worked in darning stitch and contained by an outlining thread, or Drawnworks by overcasting the mesh sides so that the gauze weave was no longer visible.

◇MATERIALS   The silk gauzes available today are not only over-stiffened, but the wefts tend to be twice as thick as the warps. The contrast between double warps and single wefts is, therefore, eliminated and the fabric is scarcely distinguishable from a fine canvas.

A thick soft thread is very effective and speeds the work. Harmonizing shades of colour can be used. Thinner tightly-spun threads give a harder appearance.

A blunt-tipped needle.

An embroidery frame, preferably square.

◇STITCHES   Running stitches in a horizontal direction. They can be varied in several ways: (a) passing in and out of every mesh; (b) passing over and under a variable number of meshes; (c) taking the thread once, twice or three times through each mesh (fig. 103).

FIG. 103a

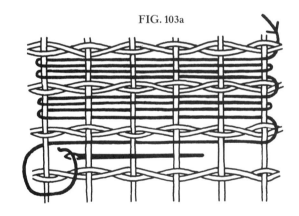

103a-d *Stitches used in Buratto.*
103a *The commonest stitch in Buratto. Simple running stitches passing over and under alternate wefts are taken back and forth across the area to be filled in.*
103b *Satin stitch. Used only in very large pieces to make huge designs.* (cont. overleaf.)

FIG. 103b

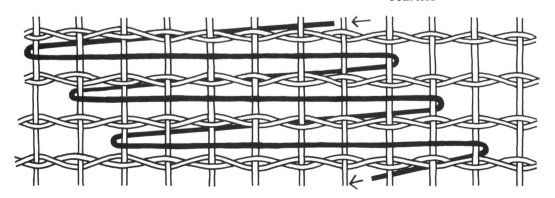

FIG. 103c

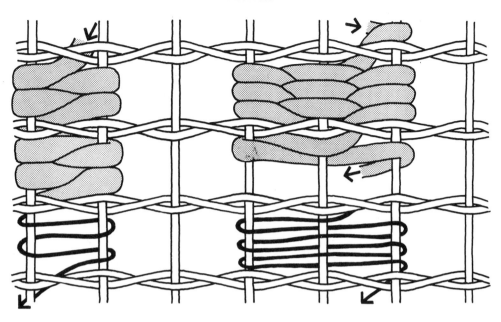

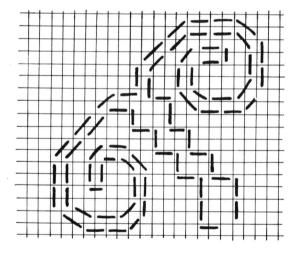

FIG. 103d

103c *The needleweaving effect over a column of two or three wefts. Above: the appearance in the actual lace. Below: the course taken by the thread.*
103d *A vine leaf tendril from a seventeenth-century Buratto lace, showing a curved effect, produced by a mixture of diagonal and straight stitches passing in and out of the meshes. The blank area within the tendril and stem will be filled with stitches.*

Opposite Buratto. **Top** A heavy linen flounce designed with horses and griffins. **Below** Natural-coloured silk gauze with angels in an attitude of prayer; a linen flounce with baroque flowers, closely darned, and outlined with thicker thread, all seventeenth century, Italian. **Centre** peacocks in white running stitches on a blue ground, nineteenth century.
Page 118 Limerick run lace. Detail of a collar, and flounce, both on square net, showing traditional harps and shamrock.

The pattern

Fig. 104 shows a simple seventeenth-century design, which is worked by counting the meshes. If preferred, use a pencil to mark the outline of the design on the gauze.

Filling in the stitches

The blank portions of fig. 104 are to be filled with running stitches. The grid represents the meshes which will remain visible when the lace is complete. The instructions given below suggest types of stitches to be used and an order for working. If several colours are used, neatly knot

the new thread to the old on the reverse side. The skill required in Buratto is to keep the stitches flat and the tension even.

Begin at the lower left-hand corner of A. Using the stitch shown in fig. 103a, work two rows of meshes. According to the thickness of the thread, it may pass once, twice or three times through each mesh.

Take the thread through the stitches at the

104 *The design.*
Gridded areas = plain gauze
Blank areas = to be filled with running stitches

FIG. 104

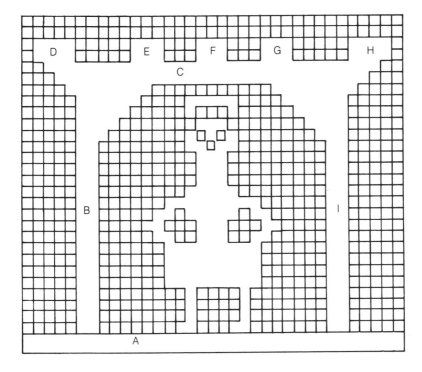

Page 119 Run Laces. **Below** A French provincial bonnet, its flounce held in a crimping iron. **Clockwise from bottom left** a Limerick stole, black embroidery on round net; a poke bonnet veil; imitation Spanish blonde in black silk; two Limerick stoles in cotton; a silk stole resembling the blonde bobbin lace of Caen; a brass needle case with knob-tipped needle. Mid-nineteenth century.
Opposite Carrickmacross. **Top left** A partly worked pattern; Carrickmacross guipure. **Right** a shawl collar with chain-stitching; a bertha collar with couched cord. **Centre** a handkerchief, the exposed net filled with decorative running stitches. **Left** a veil of net-on-net appliqué. Nineteenth century.

back of row 2 to mesh 6, the beginning of column B. The column is two meshes wide. Work all the way up it in a needleweaving manner (fig. 103c).

The widening top of B passes into the arch C. In these areas a modified fig. 103b stitch can be used, with the surface thread passing over two, three or more meshes, then under one. C consists of two mesh rows. End below D.

Each of the battlements D, E, F, G and H can be worked in satin-stitch (fig. 103b, but aligned

exactly above each other). Take the thread through the back of the stitches from D to E, E to F, F to G, and G to H.

Work the wide top of I and its narrow column so that it matches B. Continue downwards until you meet the ground A.

Work the figure in running stitches of your choice. If desired, the figure and the archway can be outlined in double running stitch (known as Holbein stitch) which will give a continuous border (fig. 105).

FIG. 105

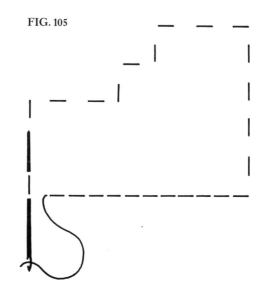

105 *Holbein stitch. Make small evenly spaced running stitches around the outline. Work round a second time, alternating the stitches so that all the gaps are filled in. In practice the needle would use the same holes each time. Here the stitches have been spaced to make the technique clearer. The needle is passing immediately underneath a stitch of the first row.*

11
LIMERICK

◇◇◇

*R*UN LACES are also known as needlerun or darned net. They consist of machine nets embroidered in a variety of running stitches.

◇HISTORY Running stitches as such were used from early times to decorate: (a) filet, a plain square-meshed knotted net; (b) Buratto, a plain square-meshed woven gauze (Chapter 10); (c) Drawnwork, an open fabric made by the removal or displacement of warp and/or weft threads (Chapter 1).

However, the date of commencement of run laces as defined above is obscure. Running stitches were added to the silk weft- and warp-knitted nets of c.1780 to 1830, though tambour decoration was considerably more frequent. A report by Felkin in 1831 states that one half of England's production of 'bobbin-net' was exported in a plain state and 'embroidered chiefly in Belgium, Saxony and, until recent events, in ill-fated Poland'. This implies that the industry was already well established. Indeed, he says that 'but for the high rate of wages in this country' – namely one shilling (5p) a day for 'splendid silk shawls' on each of which the women had to work fourteen hours a day, six days a week, for a six-week period – 'much of the work which thus falls into the hands of foreign embroiderers would be executed at home'.

Bobbinet, or twist net, was invented by John Heathcoat in 1809 as a two-twist or round-mesh form. Only this 'round' bobbinet existed until the early 1830s when a 'square' or four-twist net was invented (fig. 106). Production of the square net, which was lighter in appearance, but more expensive and liable to pull out of shape, ended in the 1960s. Thus early run laces would be worked on round net; from c.1830 to the 1960s on either round or square; and since then on round only.

◇DISTRIBUTION The original geographical location of run laces was almost certainly England, where machine nets were invented. Net machines however were promptly smuggled into France, and one of the first mentions of embroidered bobbinet was in 1816, a dress made in Douay for the Duchesse d'Angoulême, Marie Antoinette's daughter. Many references are ambiguous since 'embroidered net ' covers not only needlerun, but also tambour work and fabric appliqué (Chapter 12).

Workers specializing in needlerun were called 'runners', and large

FIG. 106a

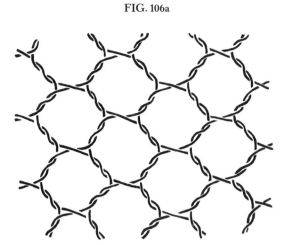

FIG. 106b

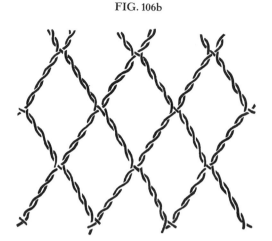

106a *Two-twist or round mesh. Depending on the tension, the hole will appear slightly elongated in the vertical direction shown.*

106b *Four-twist, square or diamond mesh, sometimes known as Brussels net. In arranging the net for run embroidery, the meshes are usually arranged with the longer axis vertical, that is with the crossed threads aligned at the top and bottom. In a four-sided object, such as a veil, the mesh will be elongated vertically on two sides of the square, and horizontally on the other two.*

numbers of women and children were employed as outworkers. The number diminished drastically, however, after the Jacquard automatic patterning device was applied to Pusher and Leavers lace machines in the 1840s. Nottingham was an early centre, and the technique spread from there to Limerick in Ireland, which became famous for the fineness of its linen thread and the variety of stitches used. The flowers were often delineated by a heavier run-in thread or by an outline of tamboured chain-stitching. Limerick work deteriorated during the 1850s. From being professionally commercial and supervised, it was dispersed to remote cottages isolated from any form of easy communication. The rate of pay dropped: by the 1880s it was 1d (less than half of a decimal penny) per day, for ten hours work, which was scarcely an enticement. According to *The Times* in 1904, 'Limerick Lace' was greatly in demand for ball and evening gowns, and for afternoon dresses, but this is likely to mean tambour work, not needle-run.

Commercial run laces of the nineteenth and early twentieth centuries were also associated with: Lunéville, where the run decoration was supplemented by satin-stitch flowers worked over a padded core; Barcelona, where bobbin-lace Spanish blondes were simulated by plain running stitches in heavy black silk on black tulle, with neither outline nor fancy stitch decoration; Delhi laces of northern India, where cone designs and flowers were brilliantly embroidered in coloured floss silks on nets dyed red or black; and Brittany's Bretonne laces in which stem and satin stitches largely replaced the run technique, and buttonhole stitches the bordering picots.

◇MATERIALS For Limerick run lace.

Net: this can be round- or square-meshed bobbinet made of cotton, or Raschel net of man-made fibre.

Embroidery thread: cotton or linen thread for the bobbinet; nylon or other synthetic thread for the Raschel. Two different thicknesses can be used to give variety of effect.

Sewing needle with a slightly blunted tip, or a crewel needle used eye first.

Circular or square embroidery frame to hold the net firmly as it is worked.

Stiletto, in some stitches, to enlarge the mesh holes. Picot edging for finishing the sides of the net.

A design inked, transferred, painted or photocopied onto a suitable card. White or yellow glazed calico is traditional, but it is not essential for the pattern card or cloth to be coloured. The outlining stitches will be made over a dark line, and this will show them up with sufficient clarity. Only the outline needs to be shown; varied filling stitches can be indicated by numbers.

◇STITCHES Assorted run stitches only, but over fifty exist. Older Limerick laces sometimes show forty fillings in a single piece. Darning stitches may be used instead of running for the plainer areas of the design.

The design
Fig. 107 shows a simple spray of leaves, tendrils and small star-shaped flowers. This can be repeated to make the border of a wedding veil, while sprigs based on the same theme are worked at regular intervals across the centre.

Setting up the work.
Fix the net in the embroidery frame, taking care (a) to get it straight (fig. 106); and (b) not to stretch it too tightly since this will cause a balloon-ing effect which will gradually spread all over the veil as one part after another is fixed progressively to the frame – the result is novel and interesting, but undesirable.

The pattern is only needed to make the shapes identical. First run a coloured guide thread in a straight line around each side of the veil, parallel to the edge so that the sprays will be exactly positioned. Then, starting near a corner, place the pattern at the back of the net and tack it in position.

FIG. 107

107 *Spray for the border of the veil, and sprigs for the central area. The spray can be easily adapted to fit the corners. To place the sprigs evenly, mark out the middle of the veil with diagonal lines of coloured tacking thread, at least 12 cm (5 in) apart. Position the sprigs at the intersection of these lines. Numbers 1 to 5 = stitch types shown in fig. 110.*

Working the outline

As far as possible use a continuous thread. If threads have to be joined, this is done with a simple knot. Double strands are traditional rather than a single thicker thread which would give a less decorative effect.

The thread can be attached to the first mesh by a knotted buttonhole stitch (see fig. 108a). Take the needle in and out of every mesh, missing none of them, to produce a smooth shape with curves unblurred by angularity (fig. 108b). The tendrils of fig. 107 consist of this stitch only. Separate the threads and take a single thread along to the tip of the tendril, and then run it back again through the same meshes to double up finally with its partner and continue the outline. Alternatively, work with double thread to the tip of the tendril then overcast lightly on the way back.

The neatest way to outline the small flowers and leaves is to take a single thread along the stem, around the petal or leaf outline, and back down the stem again.

The large leaves are outlined with a double thread. The central areas, and the veins, can also be outlined in this way, or they can simply be indicated by the junction of two types of filling stitch, or by a line of holes where the meshes are slightly enlarged (fig. 109).

When all the outlining of the spray is complete, cut through the tacking stitches, and remove the pattern from the net.

Re-attach the pattern where you wish to work the next motif, remembering that the more closely the sprays are positioned the more will have to be worked before the veil border is complete.

The filling stitches

It is a good idea to work the outline of every spray all the way round the veil before you begin the fancy fillings. You can then concentrate on

FIG. 108a

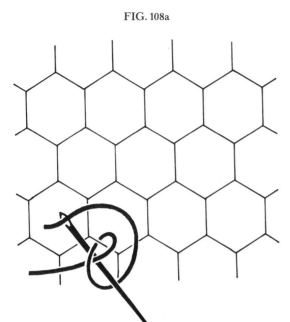

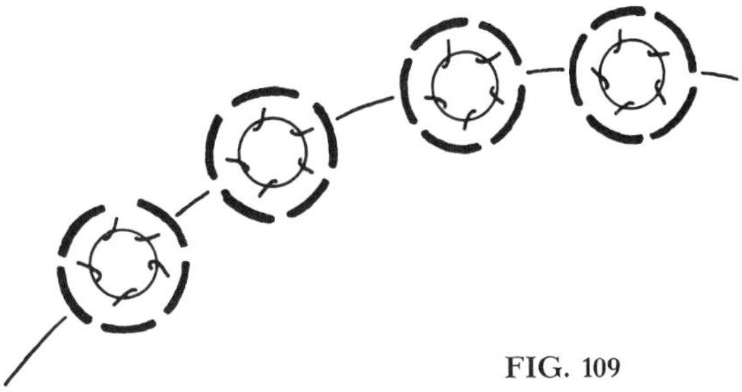

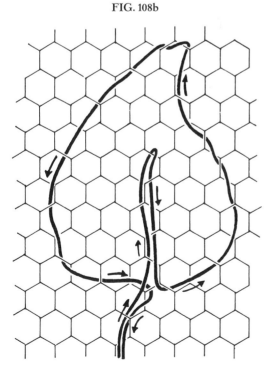

FIG. 109

108a *To make a knotted buttonhole stitch, hold the end of the thread to prevent it slipping. Pass the needle through one side of the mesh, and work a buttonhole stitch around the crossed threads, as shown.*

108b *Running in the outline of a small leaf. A single thread is taken along the stem, up the vein, back again, around the leaf and once more along the stem. The arrows indicate the direction of the running stitches.*

109 *The two areas of the leaf are separated by a series of holes made with a stiletto. The threads of the meshes are pushed back, then overcast to keep them in place. An outlining thread is added for emphasis.*

FIG. 108b

these without the distraction of having to set up the pattern again and the constant repetition of the decorative stitches will make them easier.

Five traditional filling stitches are illustrated in fig. 110a. Their numbers relate to the areas indicated in fig. 107. Many more can be found by examining old Limerick laces. This is also an excellent area in which to experiment on your own account without being overly dependent on tradition. Any of the stitches of the earliest Limerick run laces can be worked on two-twist bobbinet, but stitches for round and square nets are not always interchangeable.

When a fine thread is used for the fillings, it is taken around the outline at the end of every row. This prevents gaps appearing between outline and filling, and gives a neater appearance. With thicker thread, however, the effect would be clumsy, so the rows of stitches end within the outline and do not cross it.

110a *The filling stitches numbered 1–5 in fig. 107.*

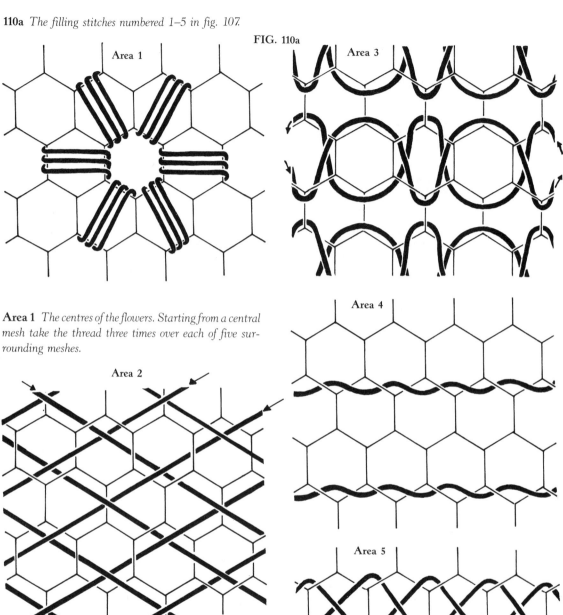

FIG. 110a

Area 1

Area 3

Area 4

Area 2

Area 5

Area 1 *The centres of the flowers. Starting from a central mesh take the thread three times over each of five surrounding meshes.*

Area 2 *The petals are filled with a kind of darning stitch, taking the needle in and out of the meshes in two opposing directions.*

Areas 3, 4 and 5 *Carefully follow the thread movements from the drawings. In (3) and (5) the stitches are worked from left to right and back from right to left in the manner shown.*

FIG. 110b

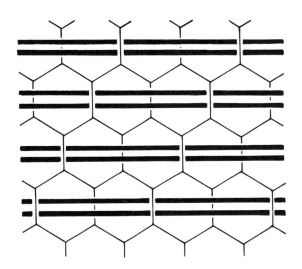

Variations

◇The run laces of France, India and Spain differ from those of Limerick in design and in the much smaller range of stitches used. However, the basic idea of a needle and thread passng in and out of the meshes of a machine net is exactly the same.

◇Late nineteenth- and twentieth-century Limerick run laces were more tourist- than fashion-orientated. For the most part they lacked the delicacy of the earlier forms and were often plastered with shamrocks.

110b *Plain running stitch using a double thread. It can be used for all the solid areas, if desired, or to replace any of stitches (1) to (5).*

12
CARRICKMACROSS

*I*N CARRICKMACROSS work shapes of material are used to form the design. The lace exists in three forms:

Method 1 Traditional appliqué. A pattern is inked or printed onto glazed cotton or a similar semi-stiff fabric; or traced onto architect's linen, and tacked to a thickish paper for support. It is then covered with machine net, and the net with a translucent fabric so that the pattern can show through. The three layers are basted together around all the design areas, so that no movement is possible between them. A cord is couched through fabric and net around the outline of the design, and the excess fabric is cut away leaving the shapes attached to the net. Decorative fillings similar to the stitches used in Limerick run lace (Chapter 11) are added.

Method 2 An opaque fabric replaces the translucent fabric used in method 1, and chain-stitches replace the couched cord. The design must now be printed or drawn on the top layer of fabric since it certainly cannot be seen through it. Chain-stitch is worked through cloth and net using a fine tambour hook and following the marked outline.

Opinions differ as to whether this form is truly Irish. It may have come from Limerick, where Carrickmacross was also made from the 1880s, or even from Belgium, which produced a great deal of tambour work in the nineteenth and early twentieth centuries.

Method 3 The net is omitted, leaving only the translucent cloth attached directly to the pattern. The couched cord is attached only to the cloth. The design areas are then linked by bars across the surface, never passing through the cloth at all (Chapter 2, page 20). When the excess cloth is cut away, what remains is not an appliqué, since there is no net, but a guipure, that is a lace in which the units of the design are linked only by bars.

Guipures had been steadily climbing back into fashion since 1851, but the guipure form of Carrickmacross appears to have died out in its pure form during the 1880s. It continued, however, as a decorative technique used to fill small cut-out areas in Carrickmacross appliqué.

Two further variations of the above are mentioned on page 134.

Carrickmacross, at its best, is a very pretty lace, far less costly than using design motifs made by hand, but quite impractical since the restraining cord pulls away too easily leaving an unsightly gap next to a raw edge of displaced and fraying cloth.

◇HISTORY & DISTRIBUTION

Carrickmacross appliqué can be regarded as a degenerate form of the bobbin or needle-lace appliqués of the late eighteenth/early nineteenth centuries in which handmade motifs were fixed to a handmade net.

The industry began about 1820 in the vicinity of Carrickmacross, Co. Monaghan, and continued with vacillating popularity well into the twentieth century, as a cottage industry. In the depressive years of the 1830s, demand diminished, but the industry was revived during the potato famines of the mid-1840s and by the 1850s was so popular that it had completely displaced Limerick tambour in fashion. In 1856 and 1887, schools were set up in nearby Cullaville and Crossmaglen, Co. Armagh – now in Northern Ireland. The town of Carrickmacross remained the market centre, and that name was formally adopted for the lace in 1872 at the Dublin Exhibition. Kells, twenty miles south of Carrickmacross, was also an important centre. In 1904 according to *The Times*, Carrickmacross lace was 'in the greatest demand', sharing that honour with Brussels, Honiton and Irish Crochet laces.

◇MATERIALS

A pattern attached to a supporting fabric.

Round- or square-meshed net. As in Limerick, the round net was originally used, then partly displaced by the square net following its invention in 1831. Round net was again obligatory after the square net ceased production in the 1960s. The size of the piece of net chosen depends on whether you intend to work the design once only, or, alternatively, whether you intend to repeat it perhaps several times to form a complete border.

The original fabric used was organza, batiste or muslin. Ideally it should be crisp, pre-shrunk, translucent and resistant to fraying.

Needles: pointed and quite strong for basting the fabric and net to the pattern and supporting cloth; pointed and smaller for couching the outlining cord; fairly long, fine and blunt-tipped for the decorative fillings.

Thread: an outlining cord, e.g. No. 12 crochet cotton; coarse cotton or coloured thread for tacking; finer thread such as No. 60 for couching the outline cord, and for making the decorative fillings.

Scissors with rounded tips for cutting away excess fabric.

◇STITCHES

Couching or whipping stitch for attaching the cord.

Any of the fifty or so filling stitches found in Limerick run laces (fig. 110, page 128 and fig. 115) can be used. These had traditional names such as cobweb, double dot, seed and daisy, but it is very difficult now to know to which filling stitches the names refer.

The free (unattached) border of the lace has loops or picots, sometimes known as twirling.

A later development was tiny circles of buttonhole stitches, either within the flowers or scattered through the net, in modest imitation of the snowstorm spot effect of many Brussels laces of the later nineteenth century. These were known as 'pops'.

Venetian picots found on the bars of Carrickmacross guipure are known as 'thorns', (see fig. 71e, page 82 and fig. 116, page 136).

◇◇◇

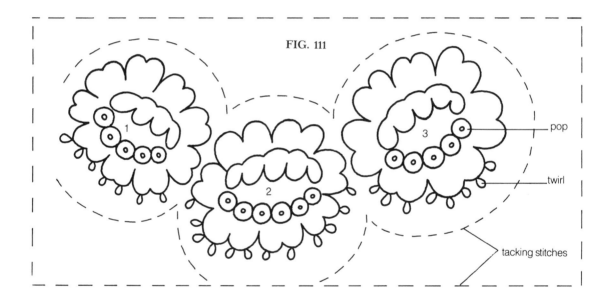

111 *A pattern for Carrickmacross appliqué showing the position of the outlining cord pops, twirls and tacking stitches. Areas 1–3 are the flower centres where the filling stitches will be worked.*

The pattern

Fig. 111 shows a simple but typical Carrickmacross border, which can be used for a tray-cloth, a luncheon set or a handkerchief corner. The pattern can be transferred directly onto the stiffened backing cloth by tracing it through dressmaker's carbon and then darkening over the white lines with waterproof ink. In the past it was sometimes traced directly onto the upper fabric by placing the translucent organza over the design and working with a quill pen, or fine brush, dipped in a solution of stone blue in thin gum water which could later be washed out. When the pattern is placed beneath, it must be sufficiently firm that the needle used for attaching the outlining cord cannot pass through it.

The basic setting up is described on page 130. Take care to smooth the net over the pattern so that it is neither stretched out of shape nor wrinkled, and so that the meshes lie in straight lines.

The outlining cord and the picots

Leave a few millimetres of cord at the beginning, and follow the pattern in such a way that a continuous cord can be used and unnecessary joins avoided.

Begin at point A and follow the direction of the arrows around the outer petals (fig. 112). Whip the cord tightly to the net, but not so tightly that net and fabric are distorted. The closer together the stitches are, the less likely it is that the fabric will pull away during use.

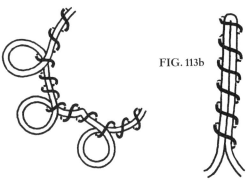

FIG. 113a

FIG. 113b

113a *Twisting the outlining cord to make the twirls. Loop the cord over itself and make one stitch around it. The loop can be clockwise or anti-clockwise and is sometimes reversed on either side of a symmetrical design. Draw up the cord until the picot is the right size, then hold it out with a pin to preserve the shape. Its thread must lie over the surface of the fabric: it is not held down at all except at its base.*
113b *Where the cords are double, such as between the petals, take the stitches over both together.*

FIG. 112a

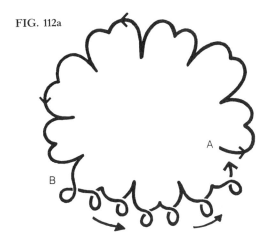

FIG. 112b

112a *The arrows show the direction of couching down the outlining cord for the outer petals and picots.*
112b *The direction of couching the cord for the pops and inner petals.*

On reaching point B, begin to make the picots or twirls (fig. 113). Continue along the lower petals, working two or three couching stitches between the picots, until you are back at point A.

Couch the cord around the five small circles, and back again to A (fig. 114). Couch along the smooth curve of the inner petals to C, then back along their scalloped edges to A once more.

The three flowers can be made quite separately. As you see the end approaching, cut the cord, leaving a few millimetres to overlap with that left at the beginning. Whip the two together onto the final bit of the outline so that they are held securely.

Alternatively the cord can be carried over between the flowers so that it is used in continuity for all of them. Starting from the left-hand flower, work out a route around the outlines of the centre and right-hand flowers, so that doubling up of the cord is minimized.

FIG. 114a　　　　　　　　　　　　　　　**FIG. 114b**

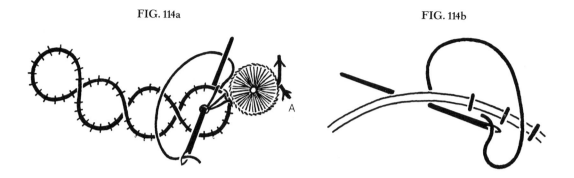

114a *Making the pops. The outlining cord has been couched and the first circle completed. In the second, the central hole has been made and the cord, fabric and net within the circle are being covered with buttonhole stitches.*
114b *Straight couching stitches are used for the circles. Elsewhere they are slanting.*

Making the pops

These can be worked either before or after the pattern and supporting fabric are removed by cutting through the tacking stitches from the reverse side. You are still working, in any case, through both the surface cloth and the net.

With a stiletto, gently ease through the fabric and net in the centre of each small circle. Buttonhole stitch from this central hole over the cord, making a neat overlap where the circles touch (fig. 114).

If circles are to be scattered over the net, they should be worked now. Separate tiny outlines of cord can be laid down, couched over, and then buttonhole-stitched over from a central stiletto-enlarged hole. This gives a rather heavy effect, however, and the outlining cord can be omitted, which makes the work easier and the final appearance more dainty.

Cutting away the unwanted fabric

Remove the pattern and supporting fabric if this has not yet been done. You now have only the top fabric and the net, joined together along the outlines of the design.

Using blunt-tipped scissors and a lot of care and patience, cut away all the fabric between and around the flowers close to the outlining cord until only the three-flowered design is left, attached to the net. Cut out the fabric in the flower centres, numbered 1, 2 and 3 in fig 111. The exposed net is now ready to be filled with decorative stitches. Four possibilities are suggested in fig. 115.

Variations

Carrickmacross guipure

This has already been mentioned on page 131. The bars are made as in Cutwork (Chapter 2, page 26) and tape-based laces (Chapter 7, page 80). Strands of sewing thread are looped back and forth between the parts to be connected. These strands are then buttonhole-stitched over, with occasional Venetian picots (fig. 116). The bars are worked above the surface of the fabric and none of their stitches pass through it. When all the bars are completed, the fabric is cut away around the outside of the design motifs and beneath the bars, leaving the motifs held together in a 'guipure' fashion.

Although the production of this lace died out commercially in the 1880s, no doubt because of its fragile nature, it was still made, domestically, in the twentieth century.

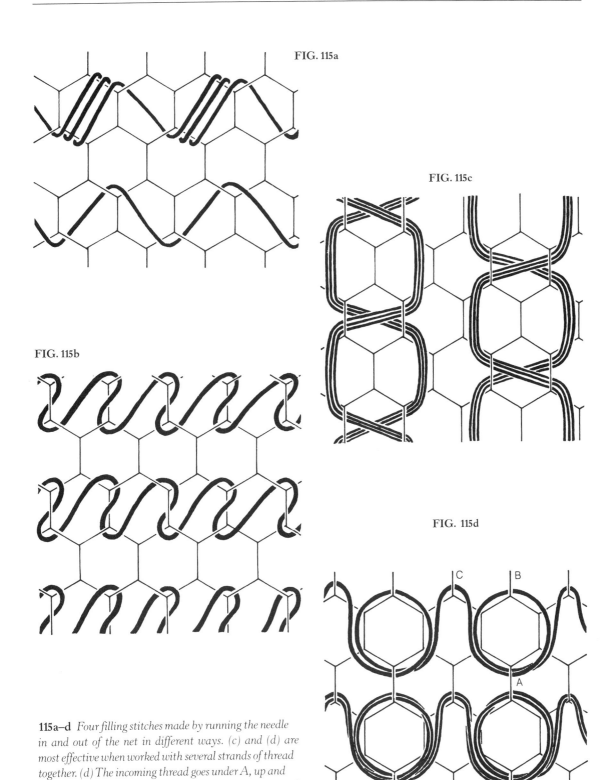

FIG. 115a

FIG. 115c

FIG. 115b

FIG. 115d

115a–d *Four filling stitches made by running the needle in and out of the net in different ways. (c) and (d) are most effective when worked with several strands of thread together. (d) The incoming thread goes under A, up and under B, up and under B, down and under A, up and under C, and so on.*

FIG. 116a

FIG. 116b

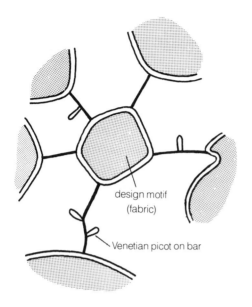

design motif
(fabric)

Venetian picot on bar

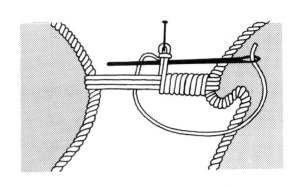

116a *Carrickmacross guipure with fragments of cloth which make the design outlined by a couched cord and linked by bars.*
116b *Two portions of the design connected by a three-thread bar. A loop of thread has been pinned out and is being buttonhole-stitched over to make a Venetian picot.*

Gauze appliqué

A woven gauze, of the kind used in Buratto work, is stretched over the net and couched to it with an outlining cord. This is very rare.

Net appliqué

A round-meshed net is stretched over a square-meshed net (see fig. 106). This second layer of net replaced the top layer of woven fabric found in traditional appliqué. The two layers were joined together by chain-stitching, and not by a couched cord. Lindsey attributes this net-on-net appliqué to the Limerick area: 'in some instances net is applied to net...there have not been many specimens though it has a beautiful effect.' (See Bibliography, page 141.)

GLOSSARY

This is restricted to obscure terms only. An explanation of other terms used in the text can be found from the index. A certain open-mindedness is needed with regard to the names of stitches. Many have at least three different names and present-day usage does not always harmonize with earlier references.

Bar

(1) strands of thread crossing the open part of a lace and used, in place of meshes, to hold the motifs of the design in place.

(2) the sides of a buttonhole stitch e.g. 'the bar has two twists'.

Buttonhole stitch A stitch with a looped edge made by taking the thread from the previous stitch around the back of the needle so that the new thread passes over is as it is pulled through. The buttonhole stitch of embroidery and lace is similar to blanket stitch but different from the tailor's or dressmaking buttonhole stitch. In lace *detached* buttonhole stitches are made in rows, each linking through the loops of the previous row or, in the first instance, to around a foundation cord. The *twisted* buttonhole stitch of lace refers to a specific type of twist and does not include every buttonhole stitch with a twist in its bars. (See Chapter 5).

Cording Taking the thread very closely round and round a stretched cord or group of threads to strengthen or thicken it.

Cordonnet A raised outline around the design. It may be shallow or heavily padded so that it produces a strongly three-dimensional effect. It is similar to the outlining cord of Chapter 12, but not to the foundation cords of Chapters 3 to 5 which have an entirely supportive function and will be overlaid by the cordonnet if this is present. The use of 'cordonnet' for the foundation cord and of 'cordonnette' for the additional raising is not traditional. It is confusing rather than clarifying, and is better avoided.

Cutwork Broadly, a lace produced by cutting away threads or portions of a woven fabric to create an openwork.

Darning stitch Made by two sets of running stitches worked at right angles to each other so that they interweave. It differs from needleweaving in which the needle is made to pass in and out of a restricted number of threads to produce a column with slightly concave sides.

Drawnwork A general term for techniques which involve the construction of openworks either by taking threads out of a woven fabric and then stitching around those that are left, or by separating the threads into groups and binding them together to give decorative effects.

Evenweave fabric Having an identical number of wefts as warps per unit area.

Filet (French). A network of threads (*cf.* Latin *opus filatorum*, and French *ouvrage de fil* – both meaning 'threadwork'). Used of hairnets, etc. from at least the thirteenth century, and taken by long usage to refer to a fabric of square meshes knotted together, like a miniture fishing net. A sheet-bend knot is used: this is different from any knot found in Chapter 8.

Gauze A square-meshed woven fabric in which paired warps enclose the weft at every pick.

Lace A slender openwork fabric made of threads (OED). In other European languages the definition may be limited by reference to techniques.

Lacis (French). A network made by the interlacing of threads.

(1) Usually a blanket term for Buratto and filet (gauze weave and hand-knotted net), both of which are square-meshed fabrics or networks subsequently decorated with running or darning stitches. But the term is also used for either, and so is ambiguous and better avoided.

(2) The plain gauze fabric used for Buratto was called 'lacis' by Dillmont. Alternatively she used the terms 'net canvas' or 'canevas-filet' (i.e. filet-canvas), since she regarded the gauze as a substitute either for the knotted filet ground, or for the unknotted square-meshed net produced on the lace-curtain machine, and which was also used at that time for running- or darning-stitch embroidery.

Needle/needlepoint lace A lace constructed of buttonhole stitches. 'Needlepoint', without the added 'lace', refers to canvas embroidery.

Needle-made lace Any lace made with a sewing needle and a single thread, whatever the stitch used.

Needlerun/run lace A lace made by running the needle in and out of the meshes of a machine net.

Needleweaving Taking the needle over and under a restricted number of parallel threads in a weft-like manner so that columns are formed.

Overcasting/oversewing/whipped stitch/roll stitch/couching Taking the needle repeatedly around a cord, with spaced stitches, so attaching the cord with each stitch to the underlying fabric.

Pick In weaving, the passage of a weft thread between stretched and separated warps.

Point lace

(1) An abbreviation of 'needlepoint' lace, meaning laces made of buttonhole stitches.

(2) A nineteenth -century term for all laces made either by bobbins or with a needle, and derived from the French *point*, meaning a stitch. For example, 'point d'Alençon' is Alençon lace, 'point de Bruxelles' is Brussels lace, 'Bucks point' is Bucks lace (of a distinctive kind).

(3) Tape-based laces imitating antique 'point de Milan' or other designs, and incorporating buttonhole stitches (see Chapter 7).

Point d'Alençon

(1) A stitch also known as 'Russian' stitch and faggoting .

(2) A needle-lace made fairly continuously in northern France from c.1717 to the present day. (See Chapter 4.)

Reticella The lace is made without any woven fabric base. Pre-made plaits or needlewoven strands are used to construct square frames with diagonals, within which a geometric design of buttonhole stitches is built up.

Running stitch The needle is taken in and out of the fabric or net in an orderly manner. It can make straight lines or decorative stitches by regulating the direction of the thread or the intervals at which the stitches are made.

Seaming lace A straight-sided band of lace used to join together two pieces of linen, for example, the front and back of a cushion cover, the sleeves and body of a shirt. It differs from an ordinary insertion in having a functional rather than a purely decorative effect.

Tambour work Chain-stitch embroidery by hand, on a woven fabric or on net, using a minute crochet hook (tambour needle).

Tulle

(1) In English, a silk bobbinet;

(2) In French, a general name for mesh grounds, whether hand- or machine-made.

SUPPLIERS

There are vast numbers of suppliers in all countries. Only a few can be listed here. For others, refer to:

UK

Lace Journal of the Lace Guild, The Hollies, 53 Audnam, Stourbridge, West Midlands DY8 4AE.
Embroidery Journal of the Embroiderers' Guild, Apt. 41A Hampton Court Palace, East Molesey, Surrey KT8 9AU
Needlelacers Newsletter of the Guild of Needlelacers

USA

IOLI Bulletin International Old Lacers, 327 Haarlem Lane, Baltimore, Maryland 21228
Embroiderers' Guild of America, 200 Fourth Avenue, Louisville, Kentucky 40202
Belgium Lace School Gazette, 1840 South Gaffey, San Pedro, California 90731

France

La Dentelle 43000 Le Puy en Velay

Belgium

Kant Kantcentrum, Bruges 8000

Denmark

Kniplebrevet Journal of Knipling i Danmark (Lacemaking in Denmark), PO Box 35, DK-6270 Tønder

Germany

Deutscher Kloppelverband e V Nordhalben

Netherlands

LOKK (National Organization of Lacemakers), Vogelwikke 4, 3738 TS Maartensdijk

Switzerland

FDS Bulletin Federation des Dentellières Suisses

Australia

Australian Lace Australian Lace Guild

New Zealand

Lace Society Newsletter

International

OIDFA Bulletin International Bobbin and Needle Lace Organization

Short list

Alby Lace Museum Cromer Road, Alby, Norwich NR11 7QE
Theo Brejaart PO Box 5199, 3008AD, Rotterdam
The British College of Lace 21 Hillmorton Road, Rugby CV22 5DF
D. J. Hornsby 149 High Street, Burton Latimer, Kettering, Northants NN15 5RL
Lacis (Jules and Kaethe Kliot), 2990 Adeline Street, Berkeley, California 94703-2590
Larkfield Crafts 4 Island Cottages, Mapledurwell, Basingstoke, Hants RG25 2LU
Lauriks and Associates 3790 El Camino Real, Suite 103, Palo Alto, California 94306
Mace and Nairn 89 Crane Street, Salisbury, Wilts.
Dorothy Pearce 5 Fulshaw Avenue, Wilmslow, Cheshire SK9 5JA
Robins Bobbins Route 1, Box 1736, Mineral Bluff, Georgia 30559
Royal School of Needlework 25 Princes Gate, London SW7 1QE
Sebalace 76 Main Street, Addington, Ilkley, West Yorks LS29 0PL
Eunice Sein Lace Crafts, 3201 Lakeshore Drive, Tallahassee, Florida 32312, USA
A. Sells 49 Pedley Lane, Clifton, Shefford, Beds
Small and Tidmas Chard, Somerset. (Manufacturers of bobbinet.)
Holly van Sciver 130 Cascadilla Park, Ithaca, New York 14850

BIBLIOGRAPHY

General
General books each covering several laces.
Anchor Manual of Needlework (Batsford, 1974).
Caulfield, S. and Saward, B., *Encyclopaedia of Victorian Needlework*, Vol. I and II (Dover reprint, NY, 1972).
Dillmont, Thérèse de, *Encyclopaedia of Needlework* Dollfus-Meig et Cie, Mulhouse, Alsace, usually known as DMC. No date but first published c.1870
Illustrated Exhibitor, Vol. I and II (Cassell, 1852).
Pethebridge, Jeanette, *A Manual of Lace* (Cassell, 1947).
Thomas, Mary, *A Dictionary of Embroidery Stitches* (Hodder and Stoughton, 1954).

For a general background of stitches, techniques, areas and dates of production.

Earnshaw, Pat, *A Dictionary of Lace* (Shire, 2nd ed. 1984).
Earnshaw, Pat, 'The History of Needle Laces: an Outline', *OIDFA Bulletin*, December 1983.

Additional patterns and stitches for the particular laces may be found in the following.

1 Drawnwork
Drawn Threadwork (DMC, n.d.).
Fangel, E., et al., *Danish Pulled Thread Embroidery* (Dover, 1977).
Lofthouse, Kate, *A Complete Guide to Drawn Fabric* (Pitman, 1933).
Vinciolo, Frederico, *Renaissance Patterns for Lace, Embroidery and Needlepoint*, 2nd part, 1606 (Dover reprint, 1971).

Weldons Practical Drawn Thread Work, Vol. 5, Nos. 25 and 52, n.d.

2 Cutwork
Cave, Oenone, *Linen Cutwork* (Vista Books, 1963).
Cousine Claire, *La Broderie Blanche* (Paris, n.d.).
Lovesey, Nenia, *Punto Tagliato* (Dryad, 1986).
Prickett, Elizabeth, *Ruskin Work* (Batsford, 1985).
Ricamo ad Intaglio (Cucirini Cantoni Coats, Milan, n.d.).
Weldons Broderie Anglaise, Vol. 30, No. 360; Vol. 31, No. 365.
Vinciolo, 1st part, 1606 (see 1).

3 Reticella
Dentelle à l'Aiguille, 1st series (DMC, n.d.).
Irish Flat Needlepoint [Youghal] *and Reticella Lace* (Needlecraft, No., 106, n.d.).
Murray, Jane, 'Point Lace From Jugoslavia', *Daily Mail Ideal Home Book*, 1953-4, pages 226-7).
Ricci. Elisa, ed., *Merletti e Ricami della Aemilia Ars* (Rome, 1929, reprinted Bologna, 1981).
Vinciolo, 1st part, 1606 (see 1).

4 Venetian lace
Caulfield and Saward, pages 454-7, 'Spanish lace'.
Cousine Claire, *Le Point de Venise* (Paris, n.d.).
Earnshaw, Pat, *Bobbin and Needle Laces, Identification and Care* (Batsford, 1983).
Evans, Nancy, *Needlelace Collar Patterns* (from Laces and Lacemaking, Florida 32312. 1984).
Hardouin, Mme., *Album de dentelle de Venise* (Paris, n.d.).

Irish Flat Needlepoint (see 3).

Lovesey, Nenia and Barley, Catherine, *Venetian Gros Point Lace* (Dryad, 1986).

Nordfors, Jill, *Needle Lace and Needleweaving* (Studio Vista, 1974).

5 English needle laces

Caulfield and Saward, pp. 253-6, 'Hollie Point'.

Earnshaw, Pat, *Bobbin and Needle Laces* (see 4).

6 Halas

Csernyanszky, Mária, *The Art of Lace-Making in Hungary* (Corvina Press, Hungary, 1962).

Farkas, Eniko, 'Point of Halas – a 20th Century Success Story', *Finger Lakes Lace Guild Newsletter*, Feb. 1986

Groszberg, Elizabeth, 'Halas Lace', *International Old Lacers Bulletin*, March 1983.

Levetus, A.S., 'The Revival of Lace-making in Hungary', *International Studio*, Vol. 42, No. 165, pages 30-5 (New York, 1911).

Nurmi-Nielsen, Anna, 'Exhibition of Hungarian Halas lace at the Rauma museum', *OIDFA Bulletin*, Winter 1985.

7 Tape-based laces

Goubaud, Mme., *Point Lace Book* (Ward, Lock and Tyler, n.d.).

Hawkins, Daisy Waterhouse, *Old Point Lace and How to Copy It* (Chatto and Windus, 1878).

Point Lace Work, 1st series (*Needlecraft Practical Journal*, No. 16, n.d.).

Touche, Victor, *The Handbook of Point Lace* (Barnard, n.d.).

Treadwin, Mrs, *Antique Point and Honiton Lace* (Ward Lock and Tyler, c. 1874).

Weldons Practical Point Lace, Vol. 10, No. 115, Vol. 11, No.129, n.d.

8 Armenian knotted laces

Chebka, Dentelle Arabe (Cartier-Bresson, n.d.).

Ionides, H.E., 'Bebilla: a Greek Lace', *Embroidery* pages 77-9, Vol. 5, No. 3, June 1937.

Tashjian, N., *Armenian Lace* (ed. Kliot, California, 1982).

9 Teneriffe

Dillmont, Thérèse de, *Teneriffe* (DMC, n.d.).

Gorman, A.L., 'Teneriffe Lace', *Harper's Bazar*, Vol. 37, No. 8, pages 778-9; No. 9, pages 862-3. 1903

May, F. L., *Hispanic Lace and Lace-making*. (The Hispanic Society of America, 1939).

Norton, Edward J., 'The Ñanduti or Spiderweb Lace of Paraguay', *Pan-American Union Bulletin*, No. 29, pages 570-6. 1909.

Stillwell, Alexandra, *the Technique of Teneriffe Lace* (Batsford, 1980).

10 Buratto

Arata, Giulio U., 'Arte Rustica Sarda – II. Tappeti e Trine', (source unknown) pages 777-802.

Vinciolo, 1st Part, 1606 (see 1).

11 Limerick

Felkin, W., *History of Machine-wrought Hosiery and Lace* (David and Charles, 1967 reprint).

Lindsey, Ben, *Irish Lace: its Origin and History* (Dublin, 1886) .

O'Connor, Eileen, *Irish Lace Making* (Dryad, 1973).

Rowe, Veronica, *Limerick Lace* (Dolmen, Ireland).

12 Carrickmacross

Lindley (see 11)

O'Cleirigh, Neilli, *Carrickmacross Lace* (Dryad, 1986).

O'Connor, Eileen, (see 11).

INDEX